Adoniram Judson

Adoniram Judson

by
Fern Neal Stocker

A Guessing Book

MOODY PRESS
CHICAGO

All Scripture quotations are from the King James Version.

Illustrations are by Virginia Hughins.

Library of Congress Cataloging in Publication Data

Stocker, Fern Neal, 1917-
   Adoniram Judson.

   (A Guessing Book)
   Summary: Presents the life of the early nineteenth-century missionary who endured many hardships working and teaching in Burma and translated the Bible into Burmese. Throughout the text the reader finds a question followed by several possible answers, one or more of which may be correct.
   1. Judson, Adoniram, 1788-1850—Juvenile literature.
2. Missionaries—Burma—Biography—Juvenile literature.
3. Missionaries—United States—Biography. 1. Judson, Adoniram, 1788-1850—Juvenile literature. 2. Missionaries—Burma—Biography—Juvenile literature.
3. Missionaries—United States—Biography. [1. Judson, Adoniram, 1788-1850. 2. Missionaries. 3. Literary recreations] I. Title. II. Series: Stocker, Fern Neal, 1917-   . Guessing book.
BV3271.J7S76   1986   266'.61'0924 [B] [92]   86-21829
ISBN 0-8024-4384-2 (pbk.)

1 2 3 4 5 6 7 Printing/LC/Year 91 90 89 88 87 86

Printed in the United States of America

To Michelle and Robin Thompson

Contents

To You, the Reader:

A Guessing Book is the story of a famous person. As you read along in this Guessing Book, you'll come to questions you can answer by yourself.

One, two, or three guesses are given, and you can choose one, two, or three answers. Sometimes all are correct, sometimes none. (You'll find the answer as you keep reading.) Pretty soon you'll know the person in the story so well you can get the answer right every time.

It may be fun to keep track of how many guesses you get right. But if you miss one, don't worry—this isn't a test.

Read this Guessing Book and learn about Adoniram Judson, a man who followed God's plan for his life.

1

Puzzles

"What is the preacher's son writing to the newspaper?" The postmaster glared at Adoniram Judson as he took the letter from him.

Jud answered,

1. "It's none of your business."
2. "I'm answering the editor's question."
3. "Why should you care?

Jud said he was answering the editor's question.

"Does your father know you wrote that letter?" demanded the postmaster.

"Well, no," admitted Jud.

"Good-bye, Jud. I'm aware of your pranks. You're a rascal, to be sure!" The postman shook his head and put the letter aside.

Jud left the post office, staring back at the large sign,

U.S. POST OFFICE
WENHAM, MASSACHUSETTS 1801

What difference does it make to him where I send my letters? I paid for the stamp, didn't I? Jud muttered to himself.

"Does your father know?"

It seemed to him that

| GUESS |

1. grown-ups were suspicious.
2. grown-ups expected the worst.
3. grown-ups were helpful.

Jud thought grown-ups were suspicious. Why should they suspect him, when all he did was to

| GUESS |

1. put stink-um on the church furnace.
2. set fire to the parsonage.
3. choke his little sister, Abby.

One cold Sunday night it had seemed funny when he put stink-um on the furnace before church. But he had taken his punishment for that. Besides, that was long ago. Now he was almost grown up at twelve years of age. "They just can't believe I'm past that silly stage," lamented Jud.

That night after supper, Jud was surprised when his father pulled out his letter—the one he had mailed that afternoon.

"Yours, Adoniram?" questioned Father.

"Why, yes, sir."

"Why did you write it? What's it about?" asked Father, not unkindly.

Jud said,

| GUESS |

1. "Where did you get my letter?"
2. "What's it to you?"
3. "Read it, sir."

Jud told his father to read the letter. He knew the postmaster must have given it to him.

"Break the seal yourself. You know I wouldn't break into another's mail," Father answered.

Jud broke the seal and handed the letter back to Father.

Father read the answer to a puzzle. "What's this?" he asked. "Let me see the puzzle."

Jud found the puzzle he had torn from the newspaper. Heading the column were the words *Can You Solve This?*

Jud watched as Father studied first the puzzle and then his answer. *Will I be punished?* he wondered. It didn't seem to him he had done anything wrong.

Father

GUESS

1. whipped Jud.
2. laughed.
3. did nothing.

Father did nothing but ask Jud to get the sealing wax and seal the letter again. "I'll give this back to the postmaster in the morning," he said.

The next Saturday Father gave Jud a new book of

GUESS

1. mysteries.
2. puzzles.
3. Bible stories.

Jud unwrapped a book of puzzles and hugged his father. Not all adults were suspicious, he decided.

When the newspaper came out the next week, there was an announcement that Adoniram Judson had solved the puzzle. Jud was shocked when neighbors and friends slapped him on the back. It seemed so strange to be

GUESS

1. looked upon with favor.
2. praised.
3. admired by grown-ups.

Jud found it strange and a bit uncomfortable to be favored, praised, and admired by adults.

Father looked over his answers to the first puzzle book and

give him another book with more difficult puzzles in it.

This time Jud was

1. unable to solve them.
2. able to solve only a few.
3. still able to solve every puzzle.

Jud loved working puzzles and finally solved every one. It really wasn't that hard for a boy who had learned to read when he was only four years old.

The townspeople began giving him hard problems in arithmetic to solve, and one day he received a letter from a friend of his father's. The letter said, "If you can master this teaser, I'll send you a dollar."

Jud said,

1. "I have plenty of pocket money."
2. "I'll get to work right away."
3. "This one is too hard."

Jud went to work but found the teaser was truly difficult. Try as hard as he could, no answer seemed possible.

Mother called, "Come, Jud, watch Nathan while I run out for a minute."

Jud answered,

1. "Can't you see I'm working on the puzzle?"
2. "Why can't Abby play with the baby?"
3. "I'll play with him."

Jud went to his brother's room and helped him with wooden blocks. They had built a foundation and were putting up walls when Jud jumped up.

"I've got it!" he shouted, dumping the blocks on the floor, leaping down the stairway, and rushing to his room.

Jud had

GUESS	1. remembered he left food cooking on the stove.
	2. solved the puzzle.
	3. forgotten to turn on his favorite TV show.

Jud had solved the puzzle.

Because Jud was a preacher's son, a bookworm, and good at arithmetic, the children at school called him

GUESS	1. a sissy.
	2. a swot.
	3. "old Virgil dug up."

The children called Jud "old Virgil dug up" because he read Virgil, a book in the Latin language. He could repeat paragraphs from his books by memory. He learned not to, however, because he did not want to be called a swot. In order for a preacher's son to be one of the gang, he had to

GUESS	1. be good at sports.
	2. play tricks on others.
	3. make people laugh.

As Jud grew older, he stopped playing tricks and tried to amuse people with puzzles and jokes. No one had yet given him a puzzle he couldn't solve.

Jud had

GUESS	1. a normal boyhood.
	2. an unusual childhood.
	3. an unhappy home life.

Jud's boyhood was normal for a preacher's son in the 1800s. During that time, everyone thought Jud would become a preacher like his father.

2

Doubts

Three years later, Judson and his friend Bailey shivered as they left their horses at the blacksmith's shop for safekeeping and walked several blocks to Providence College.

"I have to pinch myself to believe I'm really taking exams for college," Jud said.

"Why do they post everyone's scores on the blackboard?" Bailey asked.

"I guess it makes us all see who will have to study the most to keep up."

College in the 1800s was like

GUESS

1. the last years of high school today.
2. a university.
3. a private school.

"And you are only fifteen, too," Bailey said. "Most of us in the freshman class will be sixteen. Mother says she wishes there were a high school in town so we could stay home two more years."

"Oh, Bailey, my hands are shaking." Jud stopped as they began to ascend the steps of the carved stone building. "What if we don't pass the entrance exams?"

They took a place in the long line facing a sign, REGISTRA-TION.

Registration meant

GUESS	1. listing their names and addresses.
	2. telling what courses they wanted to study.
	3. getting a card to take to the examination room.

Bailey and Jud signed their names, checked their courses, and each got a card to get into the examination.

The room was full. More than one hundred students wanted to start school that fall. While they were waiting for everyone to be seated, Jud spoke to the young man in the next aisle.

"I'm Adoniram Judson from Wenham." He smiled and held out his hand.

"My name is Jacob Eames of Belfast, Maine. Glad to meet you," he said and then laughed. "You look scared."

"I *am* scared. How can you be so sure of yourself?" Jud couldn't help but admire Jacob's cocky attitude.

"Oh, I took the test last year, just so I'd know what to expect. Since then, I've studied. I won't have any trouble this year."

Jacob Eames was cocky because he

GUESS	1. was ashamed he had failed the test before.
	2. believed he knew all the answers.
	3. had studied the subjects he had failed before.

Jacob thought the test would be the same as the one he had failed the previous year. He had studied the material for a whole year now.

The first two questions on the examination looked easy to Jud, so his heart slowed, and his hands became steady. As he went on with the exam, he was surprised to find the arithmetic easy, the literature familiar, and the geography and nature questions covering material he had studied.

The examination was easy for Jud because

GUESS		1. he was smart.
		2. he was prepared.
		3. he cheated.

Jud was prepared. He was thankful for the long hours of reading in Father's library and the hundreds of arithmetic puzzles he had mastered.

He sneaked a look at Jacob Eames. *Ah, he doesn't look too cocky now,* he thought. By craning his neck, he was able to catch a glimpse of Bailey. "Hm, he looks like he's suffering—oh, poor Bailey."

Finally the exam was over, and Jud and Bailey hunted for their room number.

Jacob joined them. "Oh, I know how to find everything. Follow me." He pointed out the building where the school books were issued, the dining room—where dinner was about to be served —and the various classrooms.

"It's so big!" gasped Jud.

"Oh, you get used to it. They say it seems small before you are graduated," Jacob informed them.

"Don't talk about graduation before we even get in," objected Bailey. "I don't think I passed the test. There were so many things I never even heard about. Our teacher never covered half of it. Did he, Jud?"

"Well, I admit I learned as much of that from Father's books as I did in school."

"And to think we made fun of you for quoting Virgil. Virgil was *big* in that test. I still don't think I passed," Bailey wailed.

"If you didn't, you can take it again next year. Now that you know what to study, it won't be so hard."

Jacob Eames

GUESS		1. spoke from experience.
		2. tried to be comforting.
		3. acted superior.

Jacob spoke from experience. He wasn't sure he had passed this year but wouldn't admit it.

If the boys had not been haunted with visions of failing the test, they could have enjoyed the meal in the dining hall, the "sing" afterwards, and sleeping in strange beds. No one unpacked or settled in until the scores went up the next day.

After breakfast the next morning, the boys rushed to the examination room to see their names listed on the enormous chalkboard. The names were listed according to their scores.

Jud's name was

GUESS	1. first.
	2. tenth.
	3. forty-ninth.

Adoniram Judson was the first name listed!

It took Jud a long time to find Jacob's name listed as sixty-fourth. Poor Bailey's name was under "Failed." Then Jud went into town. He found the post office and sent a letter.

> Dear Father,
>   I've got it!
>   Your affectionate Son,
>   A. J.

He went to the blacksmith's shop to get his luggage and found Bailey and Jacob Eames there.

Bailey was

GUESS	1. crying.
	2. laughing.
	3. trying to get away.

"Come on, Bailey," Jacob said. "You don't have to be in such a hurry! Look around for a while."

Jud put his arm around Bailey. "Come back next year, friend. You'll make it. I'll write Father and tell him which books to lend you. You can study them with Dr. Dodge."

"Oh, would you write to your father? Thanks!" answered Bailey. "Now let's drive over to your room, unload your stuff, and

I'll take the horses and carriage back to Wenham."
Bailey would

GUESS

1. forget about going to college.
2. take the test next year and pass.
3. fail the test the next year.

Bailey studied and repeated the test the next year with a good score.

After Bailey was gone, Jacob got permission to room with Jud, and they became fast friends.

Jud liked Jacob Eames because he

GUESS

1. was interested in the same things.
2. was rich.
3. knew everything.

Sometimes, Jacob pretended to know everything, but Jud was not fooled. Jud liked him because they were interested in the same things. They talked and walked and walked and talked.

At first, they

GUESS

1. disagreed on many things.
2. disagreed now and then.
3. never disagreed.

Jud had always thought there was a God. He had heard how Jesus Christ died on the cross. Jacob Eames did *not* believe in God and thought Christ was only a man *pretending* to be God. They disagreed on many things.

Jud thought he could help Jacob. Instead, Jacob Eames argued forcefully—so forcefully that Jud was convinced Jacob was right when he said, "There is no God."

After four years of arguing with each other, they finally agreed. They both

GUESS

1. believed in God.
2. said, "There is no God."
3. were saved.

After four years of college, both Jud and Jacob Eames said, "There is no God." And now Jud was going home to a father and mother who expected him to be a preacher.

3

Rebellion

Jud stared at the parsonage that stood on the gentle rise just east of the Old Bay State Road. "I'm home, and life here is the same as when I left," he grumbled.

Jud

GUESS

1. attended church as usual.
2. took part in family prayers.
3. told everyone there was no God.

Out of habit and respect for his father and mother, Jud attended church and family worship.

He felt like a

GUESS

1. hypocrite.
2. hero.
3. superman.

Jud felt like a hypocrite, but he hated to hurt his family. He fooled everyone but

1. Father.
2. Mother.
3. Abby.

Abby pinched him during his prayer. When they were alone, Jud asked, "Why did you pinch me? In the old days I would have swatted you."

"Your prayers only go as high as the ceiling. You sound like you're saying words you don't really mean," Abby teased, not realizing she told the truth.

"Someday you will understand, little sister." Jud hesitated. He thought, *I must get away.*

"Father," Jud said after prayers that night, "I'm restless and would like to take a trip—go to New York—see some of the world and see how other people live."

Mr. Judson stared at his son in amazement. "Why? Why would you possibly want to leave here? Stay and teach school. Or better yet, study to be a preacher."

"Oh, Son!" Mother said, weeping. "How could you hurt me so?"

Jud looked at them—his father so tall, so domineering, so ready to rule, and his mother staring at him with wet, round eyes. He became

GUESS

1. sorry for them.
2. angry at them.
3. worried about them.

Judson lashed out angrily, "I'm twenty years old. I did what you wanted. I went to college; now I want to go my own way."

"Your own way! That's what you want, 'your own way.' Well, my son, what of God's way; do you think of that?" Now Father was angry, too.

"God's way, Father? What you mean is *your* way. At college I learned the truth. There is no God."

"No God!" Mr. Judson repeated in a hollow voice. "No God? How could you say such a thing? I've preached to you ever since you were a baby. How could you say 'no God'?"

"That's it," said Jud. "You've preached and preached and preached till I can stand it no longer. I'll not stay here and be a hypocrite. I'm going to ride the new steamboat, see the world, and work in a theater." Jud looked determined. Then he added, "I can leave my horse at Uncle Ephraim's at Sheffield and go the rest of the way to New York by steamboat. I've figured it out. I'm going, Father, whether you approve or not."

Jud dared not look at his mother, who was

GUESS	1. crying.
	2. staring at him with red eyes.
	3. wringing her hands and praying.

Out of the corner of his eye, Jud could see his mother on her knees, praying, weeping, and wringing her hands. Suddenly his anger was gone.

"Very well," his father whispered. "Go your way as the prodigal son did, but remember where home is, and come back when you can repent."

Jud went on the trip because

GUESS	1. he wanted to be his own boss.
	2. he was tired of obeying Father.
	3. he wanted to see the world.

All that was true. The next morning, Jud's mother followed him from room to room as he packed. Weeping, she begged, "If you love me, don't turn away from God. How can I enjoy heaven, knowing you aren't there?"

"Oh, Mother, don't," Jud said, as he put his clothes in the bag.

"But how can you choose the devil over God, hell instead of heaven, and make me miserable instead of making me happy? Oh, Son, don't go!" She sank to her knees and began praying for Jud.

Jud felt like

1. laughing.

"To New York, sir."

| GUESS | 2. getting angry again. |
| | 3. getting away. |

Jud left as soon as he could get away. His father gave him a horse, and he rode westward. Down the steep grade of Pleasant Street, across Town Brook, slowly he jogged on toward Boston, Worchester, and Sheffield.

Because Jud had lived on the Massachusetts coast all his life, mountains were new to him. "The mountains are glorious, awesome—free!" he told Uncle Ephraim when he reached the old minister's home. He stayed only overnight. "We can talk when I come back for the horse," he told the seventy-year-old man. "I'll tell you all about the new steamboat then. Imagine, I'm riding upstream!"

He hurried over the hills to Albany the next day, anxious to see the Hudson River and the Clermont steamboat, of which he had heard so much.

Jud felt like a proud gentleman when he bought his ticket to ride on the Clermont. He forgot the Scripture, "Pride goeth before destruction, and an haughty spirit before a fall."

To New York, sir," he said.

"Well, naturally, that's where the boat goes, if you don't get off before," the crusty ticket agent said.

"I'll go all the way, my good man," Jud answered.

He examined the paddle wheels thrashing the water and pushing the little boat along at a good speed.

He peeped into the engine room and saw long mechanical arms pushing the paddle wheels around and around. "How do they get the power?" he asked the captain.

"Go into the boiler room, and you'll find out."

Jud slipped into the hot room where men were tossing large logs into a furnace. Later he wrote Abby, "The furnace made the water boil and the steam pushed the valves that forced the arms to turn the paddle wheel. The turning paddles made us go." Jud was

GUESS	1. angry
	2. curious
	3. funny.

Jud always wanted to know how things worked.

He also loved the grandeur of spring touching the Hudson Valley. Jud listened as the passengers talked to each other. "There is the manor of the Van Rensselaers. There's where Major Andre was captured during the Revolutionary War."

As they neared the end of the trip, someone said, "That's the Harlem River going off to the left. That point's the upper end of Manhattan Island. That's were our troops went when the British drove them off the high land."

"And down there—way, way down—see, see, that's New York at the end of the island."

As they noisily departed from the boat, everyone was covered with cinders and smoke grime. One of the passengers introduced himself and then asked Jud's name.

"Oh, I'm Mr. Judson."

"What you say? Oh, I got it, Mr. Johnson."

As Jud walked up the cobble streets toward the theaters, he said to himself, *Mr. Johnson, hm, elegant. I think I'll act as Mr. Johnson in New York.*

4

Revelation

A desolate, dispirited "Mr. Johnson" slipped back down those same cobblestones in September. *I'll catch the Clermont back to Sheffield,* he thought. *Spring and summer have vanished and along with them my dreams.*

He wrote Abby, "Don't tell Father or Mother, but few theaters are open here. Sleight of hand, magic, and tumbling acts are the only ones in demand. True, *The Lyceum* does have a three-act farce, and there are a few benefits, but experienced actors are out of work, and they only laugh at a newcomer.

"I did succeed in joining with some strolling players outside the city. We took lodgings where we could and left without paying when we could. We performed in the streets, and people threw money. Some may like this vagabond life, but I felt

| GUESS | 1. shabby."
2. reckless."
3. ashamed." |

Jud did not feel happy. He felt ashamed.

"I'm going back to Sheffield to get my horse. Maybe I'll go West.

> Love,
> Jud"

When Jud reached the parsonage in Sheffield, a young man his own age answered the door.

"Oh, I say, welcome. The reverend did not tell me he expected guests, but please come in."

Jud felt warmed by the young man's smile and hearty handshake. "I'm the reverend's nephew, Jud," he explained, "and he didn't know when to expect me. Who are you?"

"Me? Oh, I'm taking his place while he is gone to Boston. I'm conducting services this weekend. It's my first chance to preach in a large church. Oh, my name—sure—I'm Joe Clark."

"And you're a preacher!" Jud was surprised. Joe seemed gentle and earnest—nothing like the dictatorial Reverend Mr. Judson.

Together they ate dinner and talked far into the night. Jud told of the world of the theater. "Father's character seems like honest granite in contrast," he said and laughed.

Joe told of his inner peace and of his plans to help the lost find peace with God before it was too late.

The next morning Jud left on his horse,

 GUESS

1. impressed with Joe.
2. angry with Joe.
3. jealous of Joe.

Jud was jealous. As he rode along he thought of the young man and the peace he seemed to have. "And I have no *peace,* no *place* to go, and no *plan* for my life," he lamented. "I wonder what Jacob Eames is doing? He never had any peace of mind either—only arguments." Jud remembered their arguments about God.

The setting sun reminded Jud to seek out an inn beside the road. The landlord apologized. "My only available room is next to a young man who is very seriously ill."

"Oh, I'm too tired to hear anything," Jud reassured him.

But tired as he was, he could not sleep. He heard footsteps hurrying, a board creaking, low voices, groans and gasps.

I wonder if the man has made his peace with God, Jud worried. *Is he prepared to die? Am I prepared to die? What if I were groaning and gasping next door?* Jud huddled under the covers. He was worried

GUESS	1. about dying.
	2. about where he would go.
	3. about life after death.

Jud questioned, *Is death an exit of this life or an entrance into the next?* Then Jud laughed to himself, *Imagine me, Judson, thinking like that. What would Jacob Eames say?* Jud smiled, thinking how Jacob would laugh. He finally fell asleep when quiet fell over the inn.

The next morning when he checked out, he asked if the young man next door was better.

"He is dead."

"Dead!" Jud's stomach turned. "Do you know who he was?"

"Oh, yes. Young man from Providence College. Name of Eames, Jacob Eames."

Lost. Lost in death. Jacob Eames was lost. All his arguments died with him. Jud pondered the thought that

GUESS	1. Jacob was wrong.
	2. there is a God.
	3. it doesn't matter.

If Jacob was right, it won't matter; but if Jacob was mistaken, he is now in hell, with no chance of changing his mind, Jud reasoned. *Jacob was wrong. He is in hell. I know it.*

For Jud, however,

GUESS	1. there was still time.
	2. there was no hope.
	3. there was hope.

Jud mounted his horse and rode toward home. With no heart

31

for wandering anymore, he wanted to talk to his father while there was still time.

On Jud's arrival, Reverend Judson welcomed his son and introduced him to two guests.

"Meet Dr. Moses Stuart and Dr. Edward Dorr Griffin. They have agreed to be teachers at a new theological seminary in Andover. Adoniram, my son, you can ask them anything that troubles you. I see you look troubled."

Just then Jud's mother rushed in and dragged Jud upstairs. "Time enough for talk later," she said. "Let me look at my boy and see to a bath and a change of clothes." Upstairs, Abby flew into her brother's arms. "Welcome home, you prodigal son!" she said.

In the days that followed, Jud talked with the teachers. "It is evident, my boy, that you need time to think," Dr. Griffin counseled. "Why don't you come to Andover, not as a preacher candidate, but as a special student. There you will have time to get your questions answered. Think about it."

Jud did consider it, and he decided

GUESS	1. to go back to New York.
	2. to go to Andover.
	3. to stay home.

Jud decided to go to Andover. In three months' time, he found

GUESS	1. the answers to his questions.
	2. Christ as Savior.
	3. his father was wrong.

Jud found the answers to his questions and accepted the Lord. A new life in Christ began.

5

Choices

After a year at Andover, Jud came home for the summer. He was surprised to see that Abby had become a young lady. "Somehow, I guess I always thought you would stay a child, a little sister."

"I am your little sister, you oaf! What did you do but turn into a preacher, something I never expected of you—of all people!"

"Well, you are right, I never would have believed I'd say I want more than anything else to please God, but I do. Do you think joining the church would be the right thing?"

"Why ask me? Ask God," Abby objected.

"Oh, I do. I ask God about everything. At school I have a note on my mirror that says, 'Is it pleasing to God?' I look at it every day."

"You do?" Abby stopped to look suspiciously at her brother. "You really do!" she concluded in amazement. "Well, I do think joining the church would please God. I know it would please Father!"

Jud decided

| GUESS | 1. not to join his father's church. |
| | 2. to join the church. |

3. to go away.

Jud joined the church that summer and returned to Andover in the fall to continue his studies. In the library one day he found a copy of a sermon preached by Dr. C. Buchanan in Bristol, England.
   " 'The Star of the East.' What a curious title," he mused. Jud

GUESS
1. read the sermon.
2. tossed it away.
3. never had time to read it.

Jud read the sermon and found it urged Christians to preach in India. "The time is ripe to spread Christianity among Eastern people," the sermon said. It also told of a German missionary, Schwartz, who had spent fifty years in India.

Jud looked up other stories of missionaries: Bartholomeus Ziegenbalg in 1715, William Carey in 1800, Captain Benjamin Wickes in 1805, and Robert Morrison in 1807. "Why that was only two years ago!" Jud spoke aloud in the library, then covered his mouth.*

Jud read of the ship owner who said to Morrison, "And so, Mr. Morrison, you really expect to make an impression on the idolatry of the Eastern empire?" "No sir," Mr. Morrison replied. "I expect God will."

After Jud read about Sangerman, who had labored long in Burma, he couldn't get Burma out of his thoughts.

Jud debated with himself all during 1809. He was concerned about

GUESS
1. missions.
2. what girl he should marry.
3. his part in missions.

One winter day, Jud, concerned about his part in missions, left his friends in the warm dormitory. He walked in a snowy grove of

*In those days, no one ever spoke aloud in the library.

trees behind the university buildings, burying his hands in his pockets. As the pale sun set in the west, he tramped and prayed.

Suddenly, he thought,

GUESS	1. *"Actions are more precious than words."*
	2. *"Go ye into all the world, and preach the gospel."*
	3. *"With God all things are possible."*

The scripture verse "Go ye into all the world, and preach the gospel to every creature," rang in Jud's ears, flashed on his mind's eye, and imprinted itself on his heart.

He told his school friends, "I came to a full decision and am resolved to obey God's command at all events."

The two Sams, Sam Newell and Sam Knott, listened carefully but said nothing. James Richards, also, remained quiet, but to Jud's surprise little Sammy Mills, who had just entered Andover, cried out, "Bravo, bravo! I, too, have decided on missions but didn't dare tell anyone."

Sam Knott dimmed their enthusiasm when he said, "It is very well to say you are going to be a missionary, but who is going to send you? There is no American Missionary Society. Do you imagine the English will send you?"

The problem was that

GUESS	1. there was no missionary society in the United States.
	2. no one cared.
	3. missionaries were underpaid.

Jud determined to discuss the need for an American Missionary Society with his father, and he welcomed vacation time to see his family.

But when Jud returned home he found

GUESS	1. Father
	2. Mother
	3. Abby

very closemouthed. He tried to bribe Abby. "If you will tell your secret, I'll tell mine."

"Oh, no, you always got me to 'tell' when I was little, but this time you will wait." Abby's eyes gleamed. "It's about your future." In the end, Abby

GUESS	1. told the secret.
	2. didn't tell.
	3. ran away.

"Your eyes are popping out like a bird that has just swallowed a large worm? Abby, come on, tell me!"

Abby just shook her head, smiling. "It's about your future. You will be so pleased!" Then she turned and ran away.

She's afraid she will tell, Jud thought, gazing after her slight figure. Then something akin to fear gripped him. "My future. But I know my future—missions in the East!" he murmured.

That night after prayers, Father began, "I think this is a nice time to tell the news, Jud." He looked at the family gathered around the fireplace.

Jud noticed that his little brother perked up his ears.

"Yes, Father, I know you have a secret. It's in the air. Please tell me!" Jud said impatiently.

"You know Dr. Griffin?" Father began.

"Yes, of course!"

"Well, he is about to become pastor of the Park Street Church in Boston, the largest church in Boston, you know."

"Yes, yes, go on." Jud prompted.

"He wants you to be his assistant when you graduate this spring." Father looked triumphant.

Mother burst out, "And you would be so close to home. How wonderful!"

Everyone looked at Jud. "Well, what do you say, Son?"

Jud swallowed, "But I feel God wants me to be a missionary in the East!"

Most bombs burst with noise. That one was silent. Finally, Father said, "Let us go to bed."

6

Who Will Send Us?

When Jud returned to Andover for his last semester, he could still hear Abby's arguments and Mother's pleas. At least Father had only shaken his head and said, "An apple never falls far from the tree."

"What did he mean by that?" Jud asked Abby when they were alone.

"Oh, have you never heard the story?" Abby replied. "Father followed God instead of doing what Grandfather wanted *him* to do."

Jud chuckled to himself. *No wonder Father could say nothing. I'm doing*

GUESS	1. *the same as he.*
	2. *like father, like son.*
	3. *the kind of thing he did.*

A rousing spirit seemed to prevail at Andover in 1810. The two Sams announced their intention to become missionaries and joined Jud in praying for someone to send them. Many others, led by Sammy Mills, wrote letters to churches.

As a result of the prayer and the letters, Jud was elected to present an idea for a new foreign missionary organization, which would

GUESS	1. spread information.
	2. raise money.
	3. support missionaries.

A society to do all those things needed the help of many churches. Jud, therefore, talked to a large joint meeting of churches in Bradford.

Jud stood tall and spoke in a loud voice. "We request the attention of the reverend fathers, convened here in the General Association at Bradford, to the following statement." Jud then outlined his proposal.

He said

GUESS	1. "God has called."
	2. "Four men answered."
	3. "God will lead the way."

Jud, stated, "Four men have answered God's missionary call."

A gasp came from the audience as Jud continued. "We wonder if we may expect support from a missionary society in this country, or if we must seek help from a European group. We look to the church fathers for advice, direction, and prayer. Four names are signed for missionary duty: Adoniram Judson, Jr., Samuel Knott, Jr., Samuel J. Mills, and Samuel Newell."

One by one each gave a personal testimony and sat down. A hush fell over the audience, and soon the meeting was adjourned for lunch.

"Jud, you and Sammy will have lunch at the home of Deacon John Hasseltine. See that large white house west of the Academy grounds?" A church woman pointed.

"Yes," Jud answered. "That's it?"

"That's it; go at once."

Jud and Sammy

1. followed orders.

GUESS

2. found a large group being served.
3. strolled over to a hedge and looked at the Merri-
   mack River.

He and Sammy followed the line of guests to the serving tables
in the west front room. As he picked up a plate, Jud's eyes fell upon
a girl about eighteen years old, cutting slices from a huge pie.

"There is the most beautiful girl I've ever seen," Jud whispered to Sammy. "See her black curls and—" Jud could not go on,
for she had looked up.

Her eyes danced, hinting at mischieviousness under her con-
ventional demureness. As the line moved closer to the dessert, Jud
hardly knew that his plate was almost filled by others serving food.

"Do you have room for pie?" The girl laughed at him.

"I'll always have room for—dessert." Jud managed to say
"dessert" instead of "you." He stood looking into her smiling eyes.
Pastor Allen, wishing to move the line forward, introduced them
and directed Jud and Sammy to a nearby table.

"Sammy, what did he say her name was?" Jud whispered as he
ate the pie first.

"Ann Hasseltine. This must be her home. Don't stare at her,
Jud. You look like a fool!"

Jud

GUESS

1. stared at his plate.
2. composed a poem.
3. peeked at Ann.

He peeked at Ann while people kept congratulating him on his
speech. "If loudness means anything, all your requests will be
granted," one fellow boomed.

As Jud left, he joined the line thanking the host for lunch. Ann
stood beside her father. "Adventures are to the adventurous!" Ann
smiled up at Jud. "I heard your speech this morning. I'll pray God
raises up support for all you boys."

"Please do pray for me, Ann. Please do!" Jud held her hand
and looked deeply into her eyes.

"My friends call me Nancy." She laughed before she was claimed by the next guest.

Did he imagine her eyes followed him as he left for the afternoon meeting?

A committee was appointed to consider an answer to the students' proposals. As other church business was presented, Jud searched the faces of the audience and found Ann. *Yes, she is looking in my direction,* Jud said to himself. *She sees me; I know it.* He thought he could never remember a word of the long sermons afterward, but Ann's face was clearly imprinted on his heart.

At the meeting the next day, the committee answered the students by saying,

GUESS	1. "Two men will draw up plans." 2. "A missionary society will be considered." 3. "A vote will be taken later."

After all these proclamations, the students were advised to continue their studies and wait the "further intimations of Providence."

Jud went back to Andover. "I know I should be rejoicing. They didn't say no. It's the waiting that worries my soul," he confided to Sammy.

After a month, he wrote to Ann. "Nancy, I should like to commence an acquaintanceship with you as a suitor." Then he worried, *That was a dumb thing to say. I wish I could get the letter back.* He prayed and prayed until he received an answer two weeks later.

Ann's answer was cool. It indicated a willingness "to see you, if that be my duty to God." Jud smiled. "I'll show you love is not a duty." He kissed the little letter.

For several weeks Jud rode his horse to Bradford and the Hasseltine home in the mornings. All afternoon he and Ann

GUESS	1. explored the hills and valleys of the Merrimack River. 2. explored their likes and dislikes. 3. explored their aims, ideals, and commitments.

40

Plans for the wedding bloomed.

They did all these things and fell in love.

Jud did not mind the ride back to Andover each evening. He was

GUESS	1. riding on air.
	2. sick.
	3. in love.

The churches voted to found the American Missionary Society but were uncertain as to funds. Jud offered to go to England to talk with the London Missionary Society about working together.

The English said they would send the four young men to India under their society only if they were in control.

While the members of the mission debated, Jud enjoyed the sights of London. He came upon a jewelry shop. In the window was a lovely Swiss watch swinging from a chain and having a blue enameled cover. "I must send that to Ann," he decided.

Though it cost him two weeks' lunch money, he bought it and sent it on its way to America.

By the time Jud brought back the message from the British, the American Society said, "We don't need their help. God has provided the necessary funds."

Jud urged Ann to be his wife, and plans for the wedding and departure to India bloomed.

7

I Do!

Jud was overwhelmed by the number of Ann's friends. Ann was well known because

GUESS

1. she was a favorite with the church people of Bradford.
2. she was a favorite with the young people.
3. she was the favorite of her family.

Ann was everyone's favorite, especially among the Bradford young people.

"Remember, I was trained as a child to represent Bradford in the ballet." Ann laughed. "I told you I was converted in my late teens. After that, I gave up ballet and public dancing, but until Father found Christ, our house was a center for the townspeople." Ann twirled around Jud. "They still love me, and this gives me a chance to witness for Christ—you see?"

Jud

GUESS

1. understood.
2. sulked.

3. hated the fuss.

Jud understood but hated the fuss. He also hated the fuss of his ordination at Salem Church several weeks later. It was a solemn affair, so impressive that people talked about it for years. Adoniram Judson was the first American to be ordained as a foreign missionary.

A few weeks later the wedding was anything but solemn. Jud tried to enjoy the parties and good wishes of the people of Bradford. He imagined he saw the older women gossiping behind his back. In fact, he overheard one remark: "You know she could have married well, she'll only have hardship with this one."

Jud knew there was truth in the remark, and he thought, *I'm glad I not only warned Ann but her father also.* Ann often said, "God fashions the back to the burden. Without God, I would be afraid my back was too weak." Jud loved her simple faith and trust in God.

All around him, Jud heard conversations

| GUESS |
1. about people he didn't know.
2. about events that were long past.
3. about strange aunts, uncles, and cousins.

Jud tried to appear interested in people he didn't know. When his family arrived, Jud was thankful. "You look so good to me," he told Abby.

"We had no idea your girl was the belle of Bradford!" Abby retorted. "I couldn't help loving her on the spot. Even Father and Mother are taken with her. You're lucky, Jud—I mean it." For that Jud gave her a hug. "I know, I know!"

The wedding was

| GUESS |
1. a blur to Jud.
2. a grand affair.
3. a simple ceremony.

Jud went through the grand wedding as best he could; but

when his bride came down the aisle, he knew God had given him a gift whose "price is far above rubies," as the Bible said. Peace mingled with excitement filled his soul as he placed the wedding ring on her hand. "Until death do us part," the minister intoned.

Jud took Ann to Beverly, Massachusetts, for a few days. "Alone at last," he said. Just then the door opened, and someone threw in a purse containing fifty dollars. A label read, "For Mr. Judson's private use." They

GUESS
1. resented the intrusion.
2. laughed together.
3. were thankful.

Jud and Ann were very thankful.

From Beverly they went to Salem to prepare to sail on the little ship *Caravan*.

"It begins again!" Jud laughed as the door closed on dozens of well-wishers from Salem. "Gingerbread and more gingerbread."

"They are only being kind, Jud, though I must say we have enough gingerbread to last

GUESS
1. weeks."
2. months."
3. years."

The gingerbread did last three months.

They couldn't sail on February 10 because the ship was not completely loaded. Jud liked the businesslike captain, who was only twenty-seven years old.

"We are apt to be caught in a war and will not be able to sail to India again for years," he warned.

The year was

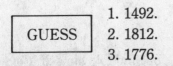
1. 1492.
2. 1812.
3. 1776.

45

The year was 1812, and the captain was right. That was the last chance to sail before war broke out between the United States and England.

On Friday, Saturday, and Sunday, the weather was stormy, and the *Caravan* couldn't sail. That gave the good people of Salem time to shower more gingerbread, cookies, and gifts upon the Judsons. How they laughed when someone gave them an opera glass, elegantly ornamented with gold figures. Monday brought a snowstorm and choked the streets so that no visitors came. Jud was

GUESS

1. tired of visitors.
2. impatient to begin the journey.
3. happy to be alone with Ann.

Jud welcomed this time to laugh with Ann. They rejoiced in their love, and she quoted:

GUESS

1. "Love and a cough cannot be hid."
2. "Love begets love."
3. "Love will find a way."

Ann refused to be concerned about the future. "Love will find a way for us, and God will lead," she said, twirling completely around with a saucepan in her hand.

Tuesday was bleak and cold. A messenger knocked on their door. "The captain thinks the wind is favorable, so come aboard."

A flurry ensued as they packed everything. Ann's best friend, Sally Kimball, arrived in time to go along in the sleigh.

By the time everything was packed into the sleigh, there was no room for Jud. So he

GUESS

1. walked.
2. called a taxi.
3. jogged.

Jud walked to the wharf. It was cold, but Jud told himself, *Cold hands, warm heart; and my heart is warmed to be going East at last!*

As it turned out, the wind died even before all were aboard. "Stay," Ann urged her friends. "Let us have one last cheerful time together."

So the friends stayed late that night. They sang, told jokes, laughed, and prayed together as they feasted on

> GUESS

1. gingerbread.
2. cookies.
3. soup.

They ate gingerbread, of course.

The next morning dawned raw and cold, but the wind was from the west, and Captain Heard said, "This is our chance to clear the coast and put to sea."

Adoniram and Ann leaned over the rail, waving and calling, "Good-bye," as the *Caravan* sailed off. The land grew fainter and finally faded into nothingness.

Ann turned to Jud. "Will we ever see home again?" Jud held her tightly.

"My dear, 'home' will go with us," he said, "just as God goes with us."

Life on the ship was comfortable, except that the ship was only ninety feet long. Walking was unsatisfactory. "We really should get some exercise," Jud said.

Ann smiled her mischievous grin, went to the cabin, and returned with

> GUESS

1. two ropes.
2. two swords.
3. two balls.

"Here, we can jump rope." And so they did, as Ann recited childhood ditties.

Sometimes they played tag to take a break from studying languages, reading, or discussing the Bible.

After five months, they moved up a quiet river toward Calcutta, in India. "The smell is fragrant beyond description; the pagodas handsome; the birds are singing. Is this our home?" Ann asked Jud.

8

Where, Oh, Where?

"**W**elcome to Calcutta!" The great William Carey himself greeted them when the *Caravan* docked.

He hurried them to his carriage, which was soon on its way to the mission compound.

Ann squealed,

GUESS	1. "See the little narrow streets!"
	2. "See the pigs running loose!"
	3. "Hear the strange language!"

Ann was most impressed with the animals in the streets and the strange smells.

Dr. Carey directed the horses away from the city to the outskirts, however. "Here's the mission complex," he said.

Ann examined the buildings and noticed

GUESS	1. no chimneys on the buildings.
	2. the buildings were on stilts.
	3. animals roved about under the buildings.

"Why don't you have chimneys?" Ann asked.

Dr. Carey laughed. "You will find out soon enough that heat is the last thing we need."

"I admit it is not needed today."

"Nor any day of the year, my dear." Dr. Carey smiled.

When they entered the bamboo buildings, Jud saw

GUESS

1. no glass in the large windows.
2. twenty-foot ceilings.
3. few partitions between rooms.

Jud noticed all these things and listened when Dr. Carey pointed out, "Everything is built to circulate the air. The heat rises to the ceiling, and the floor is not as warm."

The Carey family made the Judsons welcome and explained that dinner was always at a late hour.

When they were alone, Ann twirled around twice and flung herself into Jud's arms. "We are here! Can you believe it? It is *so* different—and *so* hot!"

"And dinner is *so* late," Jud said. "I suppose that is when the coolness comes."

Jud did not realize

GUESS

1. the cooks take a siesta.
2. "coolness" never comes in Calcutta.
3. the natives lived on rice and fish.

Jud soon found out that coolness *never* comes in Calcutta.

Ten days later an official messenger arrived. He stated, "Mr. Judson is requested to come to the government house in Calcutta immediately."

Jud went with the messenger and was told, "The American missionaries must leave the country at once. When the *Caravan* sails for the United States, you and your wife must be aboard."

When Jud was back in the mission compound, he demanded of Dr. Carey, "Who gives these orders?"

Dr. Carey answered,

GUESS	1. "The British East India Company."
	2. "The king."
	3. "The overlord of Calcutta."

Dr. Carey sadly stated, "The British East India Company. Will you go back?"

Jud answered,

GUESS	1. "I suppose we must."
	2. "God directed us to the East."
	3. "What else can we do?"

"No, indeed," Jud said. "We crossed the ocean to preach the gospel in the East. God wants us here. Why does the East India Company object, anyway?"

"It's simple. The East India Company keeps control by telling the natives they are inferior—that they are not capable of ruling. What do we tell them? Christianity teaches all men are equal under God."

"And the company thinks the natives will rebel if they know the truth. Well, maybe they should!" Jud exploded.

Dr. Carey answered,

GUESS	1. "Hush! Do not say such things."
	2. "Men have died for saying less than that."
	3. "Do you want to lose your head?"

Dr. Carey told Jud men had died for saying such revolutionary things.

"Well, where can we go? Does the company rule everywhere in the East?" Jud asked, somewhat quieted.

"There are a few islands, and Burma—that's all!"

"What about Burma?" Jud questioned.

"Burma has its own king. But two years ago, two Englishmen went there to set up a mission." Carey paused.

"What happened?" Jud questioned again.

51

"Their first convert was a Portuguese priest, who was beaten with an iron maul until he was insane. The Englishmen abandoned the effort." Dr. Carey stopped as if too pained to go on. "My own son, Felix, went to Burma as a missionary. He, too, had to flee until he married a native woman. At that time, he was permitted to return as a government worker but not as a missionary."

"Then he is still there?" Jud was hopeful.

"Yes, but he cannot preach."

"But he could help us—?"

"Only at peril to his life," Dr. Carey whispered.

Ann interrupted the men. She could see Dr. Carey was deeply hurt. "How about the islands?" she asked.

"Why don't you admit it is hopeless?" Dr. Carey replied.

Ann answered,

<table>
<tr><td rowspan="3">GUESS</td><td>1. "With God all things are possible."</td></tr>
<tr><td>2. "Nothing is hopeless with God."</td></tr>
<tr><td>3. "I guess we must go home."</td></tr>
</table>

Ann looked Dr. Carey in the eye. Jud came to her side and together they said, "With God all things are possible."

Dr. Carey smiled, "That is what I wanted to hear. Very well, we will try."

First they tried to go to the Isle of France. When that failed, the Judsons returned by ship to Calcutta, hoping the officials would not discover them.

Luther Rice arrived from America to join the Judsons and brought welcome news from home. They determined to go to the Prince of Wales Island. The officials

<table>
<tr><td rowspan="3">GUESS</td><td>1. discovered the missionaries.</td></tr>
<tr><td>2. never knew the strangers were in Calcutta.</td></tr>
<tr><td>3. shut their eyes to facts.</td></tr>
</table>

This time the missionaries managed to board the ship going to Madras before they were discovered.

"As quickly as possible leave Madras. Catch a ship going to the

52

Prince of Wales Island, because Madras is controlled by the East India Company," Dr. Carey cautioned.

The plan failed, however, because the British East India Company easily discovered the strangers in Madras. "You have two weeks before a ship leaves for America. Be on it!" the official warned.

Luther Rice made his decision. "I'm sick; this climate doesn't agree with me. Besides that, I think the American Missionary Society should know how conditions really are. I'm going home to spread the word and raise money. I feel God wants me to go to America."

"Well, I don't agree. Jud and I are not going to America. It is not God's will for us." Ann was about to cry.

"Where will you go then?" demanded Luther Rice.

Jud answered, "I checked at the docks today. There is only one ship leaving within two weeks. It is going to

GUESS	1. the Prince of Wales Island."
	2. Burma."
	3. the Island of France."

"It is going to Burma," Jud said.

"To Burma," Luther whispered, "where the only mission is abandoned. You are going to Burma?"

"Yes," Ann answered. "That is where God wants us. What do you say, Jud?"

"Yes, we will go to Burma."

9

The Promised Land

"What a rickety old vessel!" Ann shivered as she saw the rotting boards. "Does it hold out water?"

In spite of the unfavorable appearance of the little ship, Ann and Jud were happy to be aboard. "At least we are on our way to the promised land," Ann teased.

"Burma, the promised land!" Jud laughed. He looked out at the waves as the little ship left port. "Come to think of it, it *must* be the promised land, for we have been rejected everywhere else."

Only the captain could speak English, but Ann made friends because she

GUESS

1. smiled.
2. nodded.
3. crinkled up her eyes in glee.

Ann did all these things and helped everyone when she could.

In spite of bad weather, the little ship sailed. Then Ann became so ill she thought she would die. She hung her head over the side of the ship, and women patted her and held her hot forehead in their cool hands. Jud was thankful when land was finally sighted, and he held Ann up to see the gold spires of Rangoon.

"See the Sheve Dagon, the shrine built for Buddha? It is one of the wonders of the world."

Ann weakly lifted her eyes, tried to smile, and slumped back onto her cot.

Jud had read that generation after generation had built tall spires. He could count ten, some as high as four hundred feet. The natives covered the spires with pure gold every three years. "How they must love their Buddha," he murmured. "Dear God, help us to show them the way, the truth, and the life."

Ann was so sick that she could not walk from the ship next day.

The captain arranged for four natives to carry her in a chair with poles extended over their shoulders. Everyone had to go to the custom house. Here the workers examined every item of baggage and, also, the contents of their pockets. They stacked a tenth of all goods in a pile for "The eater."

"Who is 'The Eater'?" Ann roused up for a minute.

"Hush!" Jud warned.

When they finally finished at the custom house, Jud boldly asked to be taken to Felix Carey's home. The captain directed the natives and disappeared.

This was no Calcutta. Jud saw

GUESS	1. dirt everywhere.
	2. a village of ten thousand.
	3. a fort.

Jud saw all these and three wharves. The middle wharf was covered and held ten cannons. The main town was enclosed by a square wall with fortlike enclosures. "They must be ready for attack!"

The four Burmese men returned to Ann's chair, picked up an end of a pole, each resting it on one shoulder, and started off. Jud walked along.

The streets of the city were

| GUESS | 1. narrow and dirty. |
| | 2. lined with pagodas. |

56

3. full of people.

The crowded narrow streets were lined with pagodas and full of people. Little, naked children smoked cigars. Women were dressed in thin, brightly colored gauzy silks with bright scarves and gold earrings. They

<table>
<tr><td>

GUESS

</td><td>

1. argued.
2. chewed betel nut.
3. yelled in an unknown language.

</td></tr>
</table>

The women did all three.

Leprous beggers held out little cups. Even priests in saffron robes held out begging bowls.

Ann felt ill again. To rest her neck, she bowed her head, and her large bonnet hid her face. As soon as the carriers set down her chair under a tree, she was surrounded by jabbering women. They had never seen a white woman before—a white man, yes, but not a white woman.

"What strange shoes." They touched them gently. "What white arms." They slid their fingers down the length. "What strange material." They felt the thickness of her cotton dress.

Finally, they grew bold enough to lift the brim of her bonnet. Ann lifted her head and smiled weakly. At that, they burst into laughter and pranced away.

When the carriers picked up Ann's chair again, the crowd gave a shout of applause. Ann had again

<table>
<tr><td>

GUESS

</td><td>

1. looked at the sky.
2. won friends.
3. been too sick to notice.

</td></tr>
</table>

Though Ann was sick, she had again won friends.

At the mission house, which was a large handsome teakwood building outside the walls of Rangoon, Mrs. Carey welcomed the wanderers. She put Ann to bed and cared for her. Though she knew little English, she let them know Felix would soon be back from Ava.

The Judsons learned that Felix was "in favor" with the rulers of the land at the moment. He had decided to accept the king's invitation to move to Ava with his family.

"God has certainly sent you here to take over the mission, which has been a mission in name only," Felix said. "I pray God allows you to do more than I have been able to do."

"Now, let me tell you some of the pitfalls," Felix continued. "Never touch anyone with your foot."

"Why?" Jud questioned.

"I don't know, but they will hate you forever if you do. Now, another thing, never point at anyone with your foot, and whatever you do, never never stamp your foot."

Jud swallowed. "I guess I don't have to understand."

"Never cross your legs in such a way that your foot points to anyone. I'm telling you that because there is no way you could

GUESS	1. know the customs."
	2. imagine the importance of feet."
	3. understand their anger."

Felix tried to explain the strange customs because Jud and Ann could easily offend the people without knowing why.

"Never say 'no,' " Felix continued.

"How can you talk without saying 'no'?" Jud demanded.

"You say, 'Anahdeh,' which means, 'no, maybe' if you accent the first part and 'maybe, no' if you accent the last syllable."

"What's the difference?" Jud queried.

"You will find out," Felix responded. "It depends how much 'maybe' you mean. Are you ready for another?"

GUESS	1. "Never confront anyone with the unadorned truth."
	2. "Dress the truth some way."
	3. "Soften the blow of the plain truth."

Felix warned them to soften the truth.

"Let me give you another important point. If you are walking toward someone, meet them halfway. That way no one 'loses face.' To lose face is the worst punishment you can give and the worst insult you can get. Be very careful."

"Do you suppose I can remember all that?" Jud laughed.

"Now I'm going to give you the most important rule of all, dear friend. *Remember, don't rush. There is time for everything.* I was in such a hurry when I came. I wanted to rush out, preach, and convert everyone. I almost lost my head—I mean really! If these Burmese people trust you, and it takes years before they will, you will never have better friends. You can't rush—remember!"

Felix provided the Judsons with

GUESS	1. a teacher.
	2. a housekeeper.
	3. a boy for outside work.

After instructing the three helpers to take care of the Judsons, Carey prepared to move to Ava.

Before they left, however, Ann recovered from her illness. She suggested, "Perhaps I should have two boys to help. I want a large garden."

Felix smiled. "No, maybe. One boy helping—a pretty good boy; two boys helping—half a boy; and three boys helping—no boy at all."

Ann laughed. "You mean they play instead of work?"

Felix answered, "I hate to leave you here on your own, but God will bless you. I pray He will."

10

Friends

Once the Careys departed, Ann and Jud were the only English-speaking people in Rangoon. Not even Oo-oung-men, "the teacher," spoke English. The first day he came to the house with cloth wrapped around his middle and wound between his legs. He sat cross-legged before them, careful not to point his feet in their direction. He

GUESS

1. smiled.
2. nodded.
3. blinked his eyes.

Though the teacher smiled and nodded, Jud wondered, *How can he teach?* Jud sat cross-legged on the floor before him.

Ann remained in a chair. After about fifteen minutes, Oo-oung-men pointed to the kitchen and to Ann. *Ho, he doesn't want to teach me!* Ann decided.

Jud pointed to Ann and to her chair. He looked firm. Then he pointed to the teacher and to Ann.

The teacher looked displeased but nodded. Then he touched Ann's chair and said a word in Burmese. Jud repeated it three times before the teacher was satisfied, but Ann said it right the first time.

Jud pulled out a paper and pen and put them in front of the teacher. The teacher wrote the word, and Jud wrote "chair" after it. They continued with

| GUESS |

1. window.
2. floor.
3. thinking.

Jud and Ann had trouble remembering "window" and "floor." Such ideas as "thinking" were impossible at first.

From seven in the morning until the sun set behind the Sheve Dagon pagoda, Jud worked on his Burmese-English word list.

Ann had to go to the kitchen to supervise the housekeeper. She began by acting out her directions. Peals of laughter filled the house as the boy and housekeeper laughed at Ann's antics. But they

| GUESS |

1. understood her meaning.
2. followed her directions.
3. thought she was crazy.

They understood her meaning and supplied the words, so next time Ann could say "sweep the floor" or "wash the dishes" in Burmese.

The boy soon found he could pretend he did not understand the directions and thus not weed the garden. Ann told Jud, "No one is so stupid as he who will not learn." Ann made a great effort to learn "weed the garden" and "hoe the vegetables." After a week the boy had no excuse.

Ann also went to Khielly's Market in Rangoon. Here she learned words for fruits, vegetables, fish, and rice. To the teacher's surprise, Ann learned to speak Burmese faster than Jud, who studied all day. Also, Ann never failed to make friends wherever she went.

However, Jud could write the words as well as say them. Every letter in the Burmese alphabet is a round letter. "We have round letters, too." Jud showed the teacher the letters *e, o, a, u, c, m,* and *n.* "But when all the letters are round, they are hard to tell apart." Jud said it, knowing the teacher did not understand his problem.

Other problems with the Burmese writing were that there was

<table>
<tr><td>GUESS</td><td>1. no space between each word.
2. no punctuation or capital letters.
3. no paragraphs.</td></tr>
</table>

Everything ran together line after line, page after page. Ann said, "It is as tangled as a skein of wool. Mother's thread basket never looked as bad after the kittens tangled the threads."

Jud said, "I always liked puzzles—now I really have a puzzle."

Burmese writing was done on

<table>
<tr><td>GUESS</td><td>1. paper.
2. old palm leaves.
3. skins.</td></tr>
</table>

Old palm leaves were the only material the Burmese had for writing. The leaves dried, curled, and fell apart. Crumbled leaves formed a kind of powder that choked Jud and caused him to sneeze and cough. His eyes grew red and watery.

"Will we ever learn?" Ann and Jud stared at each other.

Another problem plagued them. The king in Ava demanded high taxes, which was bad enough, but the viceroy in Rangoon, who collected the taxes, demanded more and more. The more the Burmese workers grew or earned, the more the viceroy took. The people called him "The Eater," for he took their food.

"He is going to eat our salary, too!" Jud worried. "I think I'll go to see him." His visit, however, was

<table>
<tr><td>GUESS</td><td>1. a great success.
2. a failure.
3. of no value.</td></tr>
</table>

Jud wailed, "He didn't even look at me. I felt like I wasn't even there."

Ann looked at her discouraged husband. "After all," she said,

"Englishmen are common here, but an English female is a curiosity. Leave the matter to me."

A few days later she came home beaming. "Oh, Jud, let me tell you what happened! In town the other day I met a Frenchwoman who knows the viceroy's wife. I stumbled through enough French with her to let her know I would like to meet the viceroy's wife. So today she took me to their home."

"Well, what happened?" Jud loved his wife's escapades.

"The viceroy's wife wasn't up yet, so she had us wait in the outer court. All the other wives, about six, swarmed around us. They examined everything we had on. When they discovered my stockings, they wanted to find out what held them up. For a minute, I thought they would feel under my dress to discover the hooks." Ann paused, out of breath.

"Go on," Jud was amused.

"Well, just then her highness came in, dressed richly in a long robe. She had a silver pipe in her mouth. She

GUESS

1. received me politely."
2. took me by the hand."
3. seated me upon a mat."

After all three women were seated together on a mat, the Frenchwoman gave her some flowers. The viceroy's wife put several in her cap and began asking questions.

"Do you have a husband?"

"Yes."

"Are you his first wife?"

Jud winked at Ann. He knew the Burmese expected a man to have many wives.

"I said yes and told her we expected to make a permanent home in Burma."

When the viceroy came in, he

GUESS

1. sent Ann away.
2. gave her a drink.
3. waved his spear.

The viceroy offered Ann a drink and left.

"His wife and I managed to have quite a nice visit with the help of the French lady. When we rose to go, her highness again took my hand and told me she was happy to see me. She said I must come to see her every day, as I was like a sister to her. At the door I made my salaam and departed."

Jud sighed in relief. "Nancy, my dear, you do beat all! Come here, let me kiss my darling, my little first number one wife."

Ann said, "I don't believe we will have any trouble with them."

"Let's hope not," Jud concluded. "Our friends in America are far away."

The Judsons waited two-and-a-half years before they received a single letter from home. When they felt lonely or homesick, they sat down and had the Lord's Supper together. It cheered them to know Jesus was in their midst.

In November 1815 they heard the news that Mr. Hough, a missionary printer and his wife, would be joining them soon. Ann rejoiced. "What fun to have Christian fellowship once more."

11

Golden Foot

While Ann and Jud were studying the language in Burma, Luther Rice stirred up the people in America to help them. One church sent twelve small slates and chalk. Other churches sent

GUESS	1. money. 2. missionaries. 3. music.

Other churches sent money, and now two new missionaries arrived.

The Houghs brought a printing press, and at last Jud was able to get printed the two tracts he had written in Burmese. In short order, Hough put out two thousand copies. Ann had written a small catechism, which Hough printed in no time. To the Judsons, who had worked three years to achieve the language, such speed was amazing.

Ann advised Mrs. Hough, "If you will adopt the flowing silk robes of the Burmese women, you will be much cooler and more comfortable."

Jud finished his grammar of the Burmese language, including

his Burmese-English word list. Hough immediately put it into print, while Judson started to translate the gospel of Matthew. Since Hough could print faster than Jud could translate, he took the tracts to Rangoon and gave many away. All men in Burma could read, so they received the written word eagerly.

Burmese people began

GUESS	1. coming to the house.
	2. asking about Jesus.
	3. begging for more tracts.

One man came to the house asking how long it would take him to learn the religion of Jesus. Jud was delighted to teach, explain, and help him to know Christ.

Unknown to Jud, though, the king in Ava had had trouble with some Catholic priests and encouraged the viceroys to stamp out the Jesus religion.

Ann's friend had moved to Ava with her viceroy husband, and the new viceroy had no wife. While Jud was away on a missionary trip, Mr. Hough was ordered to go to the government house. He was roughly questioned and told, "All foreign teachers will soon be banished." An iron maul was swung over his head.

Mr. Hough, also, heard rumors of a war between England and Burma. He watched the English vessels leaving the harbor until only one remained.

When cholera broke out he decided,

GUESS	1. "We must leave."
	2. "Now is the hour of departure."
	3. "We will stay."

Mr. Hough decided to leave at once, taking the printing press with him. "If there is war we will be cut off from help and find missionary work impossible." He didn't say he was afraid of the cruel Burmese, but Ann saw his face. He begged Ann to come along also. "Judson has been gone so long, he is surely dead."

Ann decided

1. to go home.
2. to stay.
3. to go to Ava.

Ann stayed in Rangoon. "We are not quitters. Jud is always faithful; I will be faithful, too."

When Judson finally came home, Ann cried in relief. "My dear, I was afraid you were dead. I almost went with the Houghs to Calcutta."

"But you waited, dear girl. Praise the Lord." Jud hugged her.

Six weeks later Mr. Colman and Mr. Wheelock arrived with their wives to help in the mission. The talk of war blew over, and Judson took the new missionaries to visit the viceroy.

They were received

GUESS
1. in a harsh manner.
2. in a friendly manner.
3. in an angry manner.

This time the new viceroy was friendly to Judson and his friends. On the way home the three men talked seriously.

Judson declared, "The Burmese say, 'Don't rush, there is time for everything,' but now I believe the time has arrived for a Christian ministry. In Burma there is a custom to go in the heat of the day to what they call a *zayat*. It is a large shady building with cool wide verandas. Sometimes it is used for meetings, sometimes as an inn. People who come to worship at the pagodas rest at the *zayats*." Jud paused.

"Well, we could build a *zayat*, couldn't we?" Mr. Wheelock asked.

"Exactly," Jud answered. "If we built a *zayat* and people came to us, we could talk to them personally. Even before you know the language, you can give out tracts."

Mr. Colman interrupted. "I see. We need to be quiet—not hold large meetings that would attract attention."

"Precisely," Jud agreed.

GUESS	1. "Let the people come to us."
	2. "Answer their questions quietly."
	3. "See the power of God work."

When all those things happened, the *zayat* was built not far away on a busy roadway. Colman and Wheelock soon found themselves hampered without a knowledge of the language. They settled down with Jud's Burmese grammar and word list. Their teacher, Oo-oung-men, was delighted to find they learned more rapidly than poor Jud.

Jud spent hours in the *zayat* talking to anyone who stopped by. When there were fifteen serious inquirers, he held the first Christian service on April 4, 1819. Ann began holding meetings for women and children. They could not help noticing that many came until they realized they would have to give up Buddhism—and for that, they would be persecuted. Stories of beatings and threats frightened many away.

Moung Nau, however, continued to come and listen. A new light of joy shone in his dark face. He told Jud, "Only the Lord Jesus Christ could save me from darkness and sin." One day he stood up boldly before thirty people and said he was a Christian.

People who were friendly to Judson said,

GUESS	1. "We warn you."
	2. "The king will never allow this."
	3. "Christians will be killed."

Judson's friends warned him no one would dare show any real interest in Christianity unless the king approved.

Then it happened that there was trouble in Ava. The old king died. Finally a new young king was on the throne, and peace reigned again.

At that time Moung Nau begged to be baptized. Jud told him

GUESS	1. "It is too dangerous."
	2. "I cannot baptize you."

70

3. "Yes, I will baptize you."

Moung Nau was the first to be baptized, in a large pond, in the shadow of a great image of Buddha. Moung Nau was also the first Burmese Christian to sit down to a Communion service.

Soon the new king proved he was devoted to Buddhism. As the government people rode by on their horses, they watched the *zayat*. Evidently they thought it too small to be troubled about.

"But as more turn to Christ," Jud concluded (when two more young men were baptized), "we will have trouble unless I get permission from the king to preach."

He decided

GUESS	1. to go to Ava.
	2. to return to America.
	3. to see the king.

Jud left at once for Ava to see the Golden Foot.

He and James Colman traveled by boat the 350 miles from Rangoon and were fortunate to meet the viceroy, whose wife was Ann's friend. He prepared presents, and Moung Yo, also a friend of the viceroy, agreed to introduce him.

But the king, Golden Foot, arrived early, and when he saw Judson and James Colman, he asked, "Who are these?"

Judson replied in Burmese, "The teachers, great king."

"What! You speak Burmese? Are you teachers of religion? Are you married? Why do you dress so?"

Jud answered politely and presented his request. The king read, "There is one eternal God." He dashed the leaflet to the ground and refused the presents. "Take them away," he said.

Judson tried two more times but without success.

Golden Foot had stamped.

Back in Rangoon, the Burmese Christians

| GUESS | 1. stopped believing |
| | 2. kept on coming. |

"Are you teachers of religion?"

3. prayed.

The missionaries and the Burmese Christians prayed and remained faithful.

12

Undercover

"**A**ny Burmese who declares the American religion right and the Buddhist wrong will be severely punished," the viceroy of Rangoon proclaimed.

Those words caused the Burmese believers to

1. stop coming to the *zayat*.
2. tremble.
3. chase away inquirers.

Though the Christians trembled, they kept on coming to the services. Judson baptized two young men at twilight with only a few present. He asked God to forgive his timidity, but he

1. wanted safety for the converts.
2. wanted to be safe himself.
3. wanted to hide.

Judson hated hiding, but he wanted safety for the converts. In 1820 Mr. Colman felt unsafe in Rangoon. "I feel that I could be more useful in Arakan where there

GUESS
1. are native Christians."
2. is an established church."
3. are safeguards for my wife."

For all these reasons Mr. Colman believed God wanted him and his wife to move to Arakan. Ann cried when they left. "They were such a lovely couple."

When cholera again broke out in Rangoon, Mr. Wheelock became ill. "I don't know if it is cholera or not, but I'm going to Calcutta. This is a dreadful place, unmercifully hot and wet with nothing to eat." Mr. Wheelock meant that they had

GUESS
1. no potatoes.
2. no bread or butter.
3. no animal meat.

Actually, though the Judsons did not have potatoes, bread, butter, or animal meat, they and the native Burmese had plenty of rice, fish, jackfruit, breadfruit, oranges, bananas, pineapples, and coconuts.

When the Wheelocks left on the next ship, Ann broke down. "We are alone again, Jud! And some days I feel weak in both my body and soul. What are we to do?"

Jud told Ann, "If you ever prayed, pray now. We have a worse problem than loneliness. If one of the converts is killed, no one will ever come back to the *zayat*."

Ann and Jud had prayed together hundreds of times, but this time they spent hours and hours calling on God.

God answered by

GUESS
1. making them feel better.
2. sending the old viceroy back to Rangoon.
3. saying no.

76

God sent the viceroy back to Rangoon. Ann renewed her friendship with his wife, and the viceroy watched the *zayat* with one eye shut.

"Thank you, God!" Ann rejoiced.

"God is faithful," Jud said. "See how He answered our prayers. He will send someone to help with the work. We have been alone before, and God has always given us joy." Jud hugged Ann. "We always have each other."

But Ann's health crumbled, and her doctor warned Jud, "She must get out of this climate. Take a sea voyage; go to England for medical treatment, or you may not have a wife for long."

Jud prayed about it and decided

GUESS	1. to send Ann to England. 2. to send Ann to Calcutta. 3. to keep Ann at home.

With aching heart, Jud put his dear Ann on a ship sailing for England. "If you need more time to get well, go to America and visit your parents and friends in Bradford." He smiled as a lump formed in his throat. "But come back to me. Promise."

"I promise," Ann replied with tears in her eyes.

With no one at home, Jud spent most of his time in the *zayat*. He had a gigantic puzzle to solve. The Burmese, who had great respect for the writing of Buddha, continually asked for the holy writings of Christianity. Jud's supply of tracts was vanishing, and the new converts needed the Bible. "There is no other way. I must translate the entire Bible into the Burmese language," he told his faithful teacher. "I have translated Matthew to Ephesians, but that is only a beginning."

"I will help you if I can," Oo-oung-men replied.

Without a printing press, the teacher spent his time copying the tracts or Matthew, while Jud talked with people. A few ventured onto the veranda to ask questions each day.

The government men rode by but never stopped. *What could one poor soul do?* they wondered. *No need to bother him.*

Without Ann, the women's and children's meetings stopped. The *zayat* was

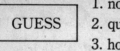
1. noisy.
2. quiet.
3. hot.

Jud and Oo-oung-men sat for long hours in the quiet *zayat*. It was hot, but the long veranda caught any breeze.

At first Jud tried to translate from his English Bible, but he was always questioning the meanings and turning to his

GUESS
1. Greek Bible.
2. Latin Bible.
3. German Bible.

While at the university, Jud had studied Greek because it was required. Now he was thankful he could turn to his Greek Bible. Soon he found he was translating from Greek to Burmese. For some reason the work went faster that way. It was good that Jud had quiet, happy days. It prepared him for the horrors ahead.

When he couldn't think of a Burmese word for a certain meaning, he would turn to his teacher for help. "It is a puzzle, I know, but I must do it!"

Sometimes they stopped work and

GUESS
1. took a break.
2. ran around the *zayat*.
3. talked.

"Did you know Aung Min died?" the teacher asked one day as they talked.

"No. His soul is lost, I think," said Jud.

"Why so?"

"He did not believe in Christ," Jud replied.

"How do you know?"

"You know a tree by its fruit or leaves, yes? You do not see the roots, but you know, if no roots, no leaves or fruit," Jud went on. "This man did not say anything about Christ. He did not pray to

Jesus. He had no fruit—not even leaves."

The teacher was amazed. "Then anyone not believing in Christ is lost?"

"Yes, all, whether Burmese or foreigners," Jud agreed.

"This is hard!"

"Yes, if it were not hard, I would never have come all this way to tell you of Jesus."

"I always wondered why you came and why you work until your eyes run water on these puzzles. But why are the white men so fortunate to know this?"

"Are not all men sinners, whether they be white or black or brown?" Jud asked. "Do not all men deserve punishment in a future state?"

"Yes, Buddha teaches that. We go to a better incarnation if we are good and a worse new life on earth if we are bad."

"Buddha says there is *no* escape," Jud pointed out. "But there *is* a way of escape. Jesus Christ took man's punishment on Himself. He took all our sins, *all* our punishment."

"Then what must man do?" the teacher asked.

"All a man has to do is to *believe* that Christ did it for him. Then, when he dies, he goes to heaven," Jud explained.

"Oh," Oo-oung-men laughed. "That is too easy! I could never believe that."

13

The Golden Favor

Jud had almost finished translating the New Testament when he received a letter from Ann.

"Dear husband,

The doctors in England recommend a year's rest in the healthful New England climate, so I am going on to America. Pray for me."

Jud swallowed his tears and blinked his eyes before he could finish reading the letter.

"Oh, God, help me in my loneliness!" he cried.

God answered his prayer by

GUESS

1. sending a child.
2. sending another missionary.
3. saying no.

God answered by sending Dr. Price as a medical missionary.

Word soon spread to the ears of the king. To Jud's surprise, a royal messenger came to Rangoon and demanded, "Dr. Price is commanded to present himself to the king."

"But I do not know the language," Dr. Price said in English. Jud translated his words to the messenger.

"Then both of you come," the messenger concluded.
With a great flurry, the men

GUESS	1. tramped 350 miles.
	2. put on their finest clothes.
	3. prepared presents.

Jud and Dr. Price traveled 350 miles by boat and approached the golden throne with awe.

The king welcomed Dr. Price and asked Jud if any Burmese had become Christians.

"Yes, a few!" Jud could not lie.

The king then ordered, "Let us hear how you preach!"

So before the entire royal court, Jud preached the gospel. He felt God had sent him to Burma for this opportunity.

To Jud's delight the king

GUESS	1. gave him some land.
	2. invited him to move to Ava.
	3. promised to build him a house.

The king promised all those things. He said Jud could preach in Ava if Dr. Price would practice medicine at his court.

Jud answered,

GUESS	1. "I will come at once."
	2. "I cannot come until my wife returns."
	3. "Dr. Price is free to decide for himself."

Jud agreed to come when Dr. Price decided to stay at the royal court. "As for myself, I cannot come until my wife returns from America. Then I will gladly accept your gifts."

Jud glowed with the good feeling of being in favor with the king.

Back in Rangoon, he increased the number of preaching services and noticed the government men had stopped riding in front of the *zayat*. The church flourished as Christians forgot their fears, and interested people dared attend the meetings.

"You will be pleased to see all these new believers," Jud wrote to Ann. "Come home as soon as possible. It seems all our hopes and dreams are to come true."

When Ann arrived on December 5, 1823, Jud was overcome. "My dear, you look like the rosy young girl I first met."

Ann twirled three times. "I feel the same, too. Let me tell you what happened in America."

Ann told Jud of her visits to churches from Massachusetts to Georgia. Everyone wanted to

GUESS	1. hear of their work.
	2. send gifts.
	3. send more missionaries.

Ann reported all these things and introduced Jud to Mr. and Mrs. Wade, who had returned with her.

"How wonderful!" Jud said. "The Wades can carry on here while we go to Ava."

"To Ava!" Ann answered. "Tell me all about it firsthand. Your letters sounded like a dream."

"There is no time to be lost. Don't unpack; we can take our things and be on our way!" Jud directed.

So they loaded everything necessary into boats and set out on their 350-mile journey up the peaceful Irrawaddy River.

Ann exclaimed, "How wonderful to get into loose silk robes again. I thought I'd choke in those stylish corsets."

When they were still a hundred miles from Ava, they heard the news.

GUESS	1. The king was dead.
	2. Burma and England were at war.
	3. Dr. Price had married.

The news was that Burma and England were at war.

When the Judsons neared Ava, Dr. Price met them. "I'm afraid

83

we are out of favor with the king," he said.

Nevertheless, Jud

GUESS	1. located the gift of land. 2. built a house. 3. went to court.

Jud organized workmen to build a home with three small rooms and a veranda on his gift of land. They were just getting settled when

GUESS	1. the English captured Rangoon. 2. the Burmese defeated England. 3. Ava was captured.

The English captured Rangoon, and the king looked around for someone to blame.

Six months after her arrival from America, as Ann cooked supper,

GUESS	1. an officer rushed in. 2. several Burmese came in. 3. a man painted with spots arrived.

"Where is the teacher?" the officer shouted loudly, directing the Burmese men and the spotted one to stand aside.

Judson stepped into the room.

"You are called by the king," the officer said, as the spotted one seized Jud and bound him tightly with a small cord around his arms.

"I'll go peacefully if you do not bother my wife," Judson pleaded. He knew the spotted one was the executioner.

Ann

1. offered money.

GUESS	2. pleaded. 3. cried.

Ann's pleas were ignored, and she was torn away from Jud. She sent Moung-Ing, one of the servants, to see what would happen to Judson. He was

GUESS	1. thrown into the death room. 2. killed. 3. beaten.

Judson was dragged by his arms into the death room where he was without

GUESS	1. food. 2. clean clothes. 3. sanitation.

The death room was so foul that Jud's stomach churned. His face had rivulets of sweat running down through the dirt. The seat of his pants was tattered from being dragged over the rocky road.

The death room held more than fifty prisoners who were fettered on the teakwood floor. All were nearly naked. The few women looked as if they were already dead. Jud noticed three Englishmen, and before dark Dr. Price was brought in and chained. When he complained, he was clubbed.

A long horizontal bamboo pole was lowered from the ceiling. Guards passed the pole between the chains from ankle to ankle. When they raised the pole, the feet of the prisoners were raised until only their shoulders and heads rested on the floor.

When the other prisoners told the Englishmen and Americans of the tortures to come, Jud decided death would be better.

Jud

1. was blinded by darkness.

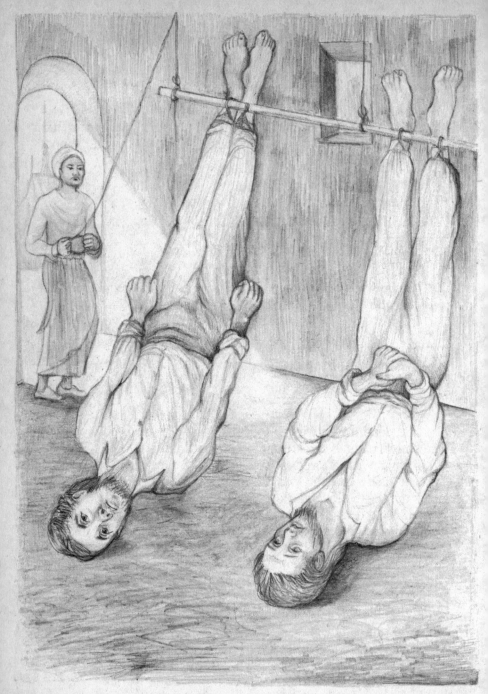

The feet of the prisoners were raised.

| GUESS |

2. was overwhelmed with heat.
3. gagged from the stench.

In the dark, Jud gagged from the heat and stench.

14
Spies

After three days of pleading with officials, Ann succeeded in bribing her way into the prison. Jud came to her, crawling from the dark room into the courtyard. He looked

 GUESS

1. haggard.
2. unshaven.
3. like a scarecrow.

Ann swallowed her horror at his appearance and hid her face in her hands. When she recovered, she said, "Here are food and water. I begged everyone to let me come sooner. Oh, Jud, do you know what the king says?"

"No. Why am I here?"

"The king says the English could not have taken Rangoon unless there were spies in Ava. He says you are a spy!"

"I'm not a spy. I'm an American missionary."

"I know, but the king says it is your fault Rangoon has fallen." She added, "When I object to your treatment, the governor says,

1. 'Your case is not different.' "

GUESS

2. 'All foreigners are spies.' "
3. 'All are treated alike.' "

He said, "Your case is not different."

When Ann came the next day, she handed Jud a hard pillow. "Jud," she whispered, "I heard they were coming to take all our property."

"What did you do?"

"I hid what I could, but they took many things."

Ann hid

GUESS

1. personal things.
2. money.
3. Jud's translation of the New Testament.

"Oh, my translation; what has become of it?" Jud wailed.

"I sewed it into the hard pillow I just gave you," Ann responded.

All of Ann's charming pleas were not lost on the officials, however. Finally, at her insistence, they removed all the Englishmen and Americans to an open shed in the prison yard. There they had air and sunlight. Ann brought food and water every day.

Jud carried his pillow to the shed, and Ann made soft pillows for all the men, to their great joy.

"Bless you," the Englishmen exclaimed. "Thank you for getting us out of that hellhole. We also thank you for the pillows!"

Jud told Dr. Price what was inside his pillow. "Once printed, this New Testament will give light to thousands of Burmans."

Dr. Price did not dim Jud's spirits, but he wondered if the Testament would ever be printed.

A few weeks later, to everyone's horror, all the prisoners but Jud were

GUESS

1. killed.
2. returned to the dark room.
3. whipped.

No amount of pleading on Ann's part could keep the Englishmen from being returned to the death room. She only succeeded in getting Dr. Price out by giving the governor a beautiful opera glass, a going-away gift they had laughed about.

Often she was not allowed to see Jud. Finally, she wrote notes and put them in the spout of the teapot she sent. The guards would take in food if she gave them enough money.

One day Ann brought scissors for

GUESS
1. cutting toenails.
2. cutting hair.
3. cutting ropes.

The guards watched closely as Ann cut off all Jud's and Dr. Price's hair. The Burmese were proud of their long locks and laughed uproariously at the bald Americans.

"Lice are worse than baldness," Jud declared.

Ann whispered, "I've been visiting the queen's sister and other members of the royal family."

"What good can it do?" questioned Jud.

"What harm can it do? They drop hints to the king that you and Dr. Price have nothing to do with the war, and I think the war goes badly for the Burmese."

"The king probably blames me for that," Jud stated.

"I think not, Jud. Pray he sees the truth," she pleaded.

"Ann, don't try to do so much. You must care for yourself, too."

Jud was concerned because

GUESS
1. robbers could attack Ann.
2. the walk from home to prison was long.
3. a baby was coming in January.

"When the baby comes in January, you must send the servant and not walk these long miles," Jud said.

"I know, dear. I'll be careful." Ann smiled.

"What are you doing to pass time?" Ann asked.

91

"We took carbon from the lamp and

	1. drew pictures on the fence."
GUESS	2. blacked our faces."
	3. marked squares on a skin."

Jud and Dr. Price marked squares on an old skin they found in the yard and played chess.

Ann continued petitioning the governor for favors for her husband and Dr. Price. The governor was curious about America and asked dozens of questions. Every day Ann enthralled him with stories of Bradford, Salem—even Washington. She told him about the cold and snow and how people lived in winter. The governor could hardly believe such strange stories.

He finally gave her a pass to visit Jud any time of the day.

"Guess what I heard today!" Ann told Jud late one afternoon.

"It must be important for you to come at such a late hour," Jud answered. "And only three months till the baby comes."

"Listen—Bandula, the great Burmese warrior, has sixty thousand men outside Rangoon, while the British have less than four thousand. Surely they will chase the British away."

"I don't know," Jud said. "A prisoner told us the British have mounted guns on the highest Sheve Dagon pagoda and have gunboats in the Rangoon River—steamboats, I mean. The Burmese have never seen a steamboat."

"Well, Bandula says, 'In eight days I shall dine in the public hall at Rangoon and afterwards return thanks in the Sheve Dagon pagoda.' We shall see!"

On December 1, 1824, Bandula advanced. The British stormed ahead, and Bandula's army

	1. dissolved.
GUESS	2. ran away.
	3. won a great victory.

Fear gripped the Burmese, who refused to shoot at their sacred pagoda. Many ran away or were killed. Only 7000 were able to retreat up the river.

After the news arrived, Ann told Jud, "The princess and the queen mother sent for me. They told me all the British have to do now is to march to Ava, clapping their hands."

"What did you advise them, my dear?" Jud asked.

"They wanted me to promise to protect them since I can speak English. I told them the English soldiers are disciplined; they would not hurt royal women. I told them I'd do what I could if *they* would do what *they* could for the prisoners."

"Good girl!" Jud hugged Ann.

On January 26 a baby was born. Jud and Ann named her

| GUESS | 1. Marie.
| | 2. Elizabeth.
| | 3. Butterworth.

They used all three names before "Judson." Twenty days later, Ann brought the baby to the prison.

The baby was

| GUESS | 1. pale.
| | 2. crying.
| | 3. healthy.

Although little Marie was a puny, wailing infant, Ann and Jud loved her at once. Jud wrote a poem for their baby:

> Sleep, darling infant, sleep
>   Hushed on thy mother's breast;
> Let no rude sound of clanking chains
>   Disturb thy balmy rest.

Shortly after the birth of the baby, the American prisoners were weighted down with more iron anklets and sent into the death room. All their possessions, including the pillows, were taken away. Jud prayed, "Oh, God, protect the New Testament sewed into my pillow."

"It means one thing," Dr. Price said. "We are to be killed at three in the morning as is the custom."

Jud felt a sense of relief. "A Christian nation will rule, and other more capable missionaries will preach here. Perhaps God will even preserve my New Testament. I leave it all to Him!"

Three o'clock came and went. Dawn came. The prisoners were kept hidden.

Ann was allowed to bring food and look into the room for five minutes. *They look more dead than alive,* she thought.

15

Punishment

Jud sent Ann a note that said he had a serious fever. Immediately Ann penned a note saying she would do what she could for him. She put it into the spout of the teapot as usual and sent a servant to the prison with the teapot.

This time the note was discovered, and she was called in front of the governor.

"Your treachery has been discovered. Have not I done many favors for you? Why do you return my kindness with trouble for the prison fathers?"

"Oh, kind sir, my husband lies ill in that dark room. He perspires incessantly in the furious heat, and the fever kills his appetite. He will die." Ann paused. "He will surely die, if you do not help." For a long minute Ann and the governor stared into each other's eyes.

"What do you want me to do, madam?" he asked.

"Let me build a bamboo shack in your enclosure across from the prison for me and the baby. From there I can easily walk to the prison. Let Jud be outside in the prison yard as he was before. I will build him a bamboo shack and come every day and feed him and give him medicine so he can live. I beg you, dear friend, please give me the orders."

The governor looked at her a long time. He

| GUESS |

1. agreed to her ideas.
2. told her to forget it.
3. said he was sorry.

To everyone's surprise, he agreed.

When the arrangements were made, Ann went to see Jud.

"I have prayed for you every moment of the day," Jud said. "When I was allowed out into the sunshine, I knew God had answered prayer."

"I was not surprised," Ann said. "With God all things are possible."

She had seen the natives build bamboo huts many times. Now she built one herself. It was so little she could not stand in it, but it covered a bed for her husband.

Every day Ann bathed and fed Jud. He went to sleep holding her hand and praising God.

As Ann slipped out of the bamboo hut one day and prepared to return to her own hovel, the guard caught her. "I thought you were to be punished for sending notes in a teapot. What power do you hold over the governor to get special treatment for your husband?"

"I have no power, but God answers prayer, and my husband prays all the time."

"Well, I'll punish you, madam! Give me your umbrella!" When Ann hesitated, he growled, "Now!" So Ann gave him her silk umbrella and heard him snicker. "Only fat people are in danger of sunstroke. The sun can't find people as thin as you."

Ann came every day and nursed Jud until the jailers drove her out at night.

On May 2, 1825, she came as usual and was delighted to find Jud beaming.

"Dear, I have good news!"

"What?"

"I have back the New Testament. I traded my new soft pillow to a guard, who was complaining about how hard his pillow was. I told him I was used to a hard pillow." Jud started to laugh but was stopped by a coughing fit.

"Mrs. Judson! Mrs. Judson!" the jailer called.

"Let me see what he wants," Ann said to Jud.

96

The jailer had a message for her from the governor. "Come to my house at once," it said.

Ann told Jud and promised to return as soon as possible.

The governor

GUESS

1. talked on and on.
2. extracted stories of America from her.
3. discussed watches.

The governor exchanged stories with Ann and kept her a long time.

Finally Ann returned to her little hut across from the prison to see how the baby was faring. The nursemaid gasped,

GUESS

1. "A storm is coming."
2. "The white prisoners are gone."
3. "The war is over."

"Gone! Where have they gone?" Ann screamed at the jailers, who pretended she was not there.

An old women said, "the Mootangai," which was a stream flowing into the Irrawaddy River. Ann ran to the river but found nothing.

After running the long way back, she dragged her feet once more to the governor's house.

The governor said,

GUESS

1. "Yes, I knew."
2. "I tried to spare you."
3. "The prisoners are at Amarapura."

The governor said, "The prisoners are at Amarapura. I do not know why, but I will see what is to be done with them." Then he looked at Ann and slowly said, "You can do nothing for your husband. Take care of yourself."

97

Jud was taken to

GUESS
1. Amarapura.
2. Oung-pen-la.
3. Rangoon.

Jud was taken to Oung-pen-la, four miles farther than Amarapura.

"Why are we here?" Dr. Price asked the other prisoners.

The answer was:

GUESS
1. to be executed.
2. to be burned alive.
3. to be tortured.

Some thought they were to be executed. One said, "See this old shattered building? It doesn't even have a roof. Can't you see they plan to burn it and us?"

Jud, who had been quiet, partly because he was so sick and weak, said, "Let us pray."

Even the Englishmen, who were not Christians, knelt in prayer.

The next day repairmen came and began to build a roof. "I guess we are staying awhile." The prisoners rejoiced.

Jud grew stronger in spite of poor conditions. Every night he slept on his hard pillow. The food was passable, and the jailers were cautious but not cruel.

One morning Jud looked up, and standing before him were Ann and the baby.

"How did you find us?" Jud said as he threw his arms around Ann and little Marie.

Ann looked

GUESS
1. worn out.
2. fresh as a daisy.
3. fine.

"You look worn out, my dear. Let me hold Marie while you sit down and tell me what happened."

"I caught a boat from Ava, then changed to ox cart to come to Amarapura. When you weren't there, I was in despair, but I asked enough people to finally discover you were only four miles away." Ann paused for breath. She felt like collapsing.

"And you held little Marie all that time?" Jud looked at Ann incredulously.

The jailer then told Ann she must go.

"But where?" she asked.

"What are your plans?"

"I plan to build a bamboo shelter just outside the prison walls." Ann looked too weak to build anything. It would soon be dark, and the jailer had to get her off the property.

"It is not our custom," the jailer said, "but another guard will replace me soon. I will take you home to my wife."

During the next six months, Ann visited Jud and also nursed the jailer's daughter, who had smallpox. When Marie became ill with smallpox also, Ann went to Ava for medicine. She took care of the baby until she became ill herself.

The jailer's wife cared for Ann

GUESS	1. until she was well.
	2. until she was better.
	3. until she died.

When Ann was better, she rushed to the prison to see Jud.

"Oh, my dear, I was so worried about you. Thank the Lord, you are better." Jud rejoiced.

"I hear you, too, have been ill."

"Yes, but we are both better. Thanks be to God!"

Finally

GUESS	1. the war was over.
	2. Burma won the war.
	3. England won the war.

England won the war, and the English general demanded the release of all prisoners. He asked his officers if there was someone trusted by both the king and the English. The name *Adoniram Judson* was suggested.

"I hear he never tells a lie, and he speaks excellent Burmese and English."

"Tell him to report here," the English general ordered.

When Jud was released from prison, he held Ann in his arms. "My dear, we are going to an English camp."

"Don't forget your hard pillow, Mr. Judson."

"No, ma'am, Mrs. Judson." Jud winked.

With little Marie, Jud and Ann set out for home—wherever that was to be.

After twenty-one months of misery, they floated down the Irrawaddy on a moonlit night. Jud held his baby in his arms and looked at his wife beside him. "I don't see how heaven can ever be better than this. Just think, Ann, we are free—free! Thank God!"

16

New Beginnings

The Judsons spent two weeks with the English army. The general liked Jud and

GUESS
1. accepted him as an interpreter.
2. ordered Jud's property taken to Amherst.
3. arranged transportation.

The general accepted Jud and sent the property in Ava to Amherst.

Why Amherst? Ann wondered.

The reason was that

GUESS
1. the Wades had moved there.
2. Amherst was protected by the British.
3. missionary work was safe there.

Because of those reasons, Ann and Jud moved to Amherst instead of war-torn Rangoon.

Once Ann was settled with the Wades in a large, comfortable home, Jud bade her farewell.

"My dear, I will be back as soon as possible. Once the treaty is signed, my place will be at your side. Keep this translation safe, for it will give light to thousands once it is printed." Jud wanted to say more, but his eyes told Ann more than his words.

"I understand," was all Ann could say. "Good-bye, my dear husband."

Jud returned to Ava. He

GUESS

1. told the king what the English general said.
2. told the general what the king said.
3. tried to get freedom for missions.

Besides translating for the general, Jud tried to get freedom for missionary work.

After a long day of arguments, Jud went to his room. "A treaty is a slow process," he grumbled. "These verbal battles are as bad as the fighting. The king forgets he lost the war and must do as the English say."

In his room, he found a letter: "My dear Sir: It is cruel indeed to torture you with doubt and suspense. To sum up the unhappy tidings,

GUESS

1. Marie is dead."
2. Mrs. Judson is no more."
3. The Wades have moved."

The words swam before Jud's eyes. "*Mrs. Judson is no more.*" When he was finally able to finish the letter, he learned she had died of cholera and was buried near the spot where she had first landed. And what of little Marie? She

GUESS

1. was cared for by Mrs. Wade.
2. also died.
3. was ill.

When Jud finished the letter, he prayed. "Thank You for Mrs.

Wade. Help her care for Marie."

The days dragged on. Mechanically Jud translated the treaty. He tried to get a clear statement of religious freedom. Finally the statement came that foreigners could build churches for themselves. Jud knew the king meant churches

GUESS

1. only for Englishmen.
2. for any believer.
3. for the Burmese.

Jud knew the king meant the foreign churches were only for foreigners. He kept quiet, however, for

GUESS

1. something is better than nothing.
2. the wording was unclear.
3. there was some hope.

The unclear wording gave the missionaries hope—at least a chance to preach to the Burmese.

The weary task was finally finished, and Judson was allowed to go home.

Amherst did not seem like home to him, and when little Marie died three months later, his world was shattered.

Only his trust in the Lord and the warm love of the missionaries kept Jud sane. Beside the Wades, Mr. and Mrs. Boardman had come from America and were working in the port of Moulmein. That place proved open for the gospel. Soon the Wades, Judson, and a new missionary printer, Mr. Bennett, joined them in Moulmein. They

GUESS

1. opened a school for boys.
2. opened a school for girls.
3. opened *zayats*.

Mr. Boardman opened a school for boys after he had mastered the language—thanks to Jud's little book on grammer. Later he and his wife worked among the Karen people. Mrs. Wade opened a school for girls, and Wade and Judson opened two *zayats* in the town. The first year thirty Burmese believers were baptized and received into the church where Mr. Wade preached. Mr. Bennett had trouble with

| GUESS |

1. the language.
2. bad type.
3. little help.

In spite of Mr. Bennett's trouble with the language and bad type, he printed many copies of

| GUESS |

1. Jud's tracts.
2. Ann's catechism.
3. the New Testament.

The missionaries found many visitors from Siam and China saying, "We have heard that there is an eternal hell. We are afraid of it. Give us a writing to tell us how to escape it." How thankful Jud was to have tracts and New Testaments to give.

As he walked down the streets at night, he could look in the windows of the homes. "In almost every house, I saw someone at a lamp reading aloud one of our papers," Jud told Mr. Bennett. "Your part in printing the Word will be rewarded in heaven."

Mr. Boardman died while working among the Karen tribes. In spite of her sorrow, his widow, Sarah, continued the work. Jud sent a letter of sympathy. Who could understand a broken and lonely heart better than Jud? Acting on impulse, he sent Ann's watch to Sarah. "This little blue watch comforted Ann. Perhaps it will comfort you, too."

When the believers were able to manage the work in both schools, Jud

| GUESS |

1. worked on the Bible.
2. went to America.

3. preached to the Karen people.

Jud spent the next two or three years preaching among the Karen tribes. Here he found numerous little churches and many Christian disciples standing firm for Christ.

Not only did Jud preach in the churches, but he began the laborious task of translating the Old Testament. "Burmese deserve the whole Bible, not just the New Testament," he told Sarah Boardman. "It also comforts me. When I'm translating, I can forget my heartache for my dear wife."

"I understand," Sarah agreed. "I keep very busy giving the Word of God to the Karens, too. I believe my dear dead husband would be pleased." Sarah caught the look of approval on Jud's face.

Jud had a little dog named Fidee. He wrote to his sister, Abby: "I have no family or living creature about me that I can call my own except Fidee; but she is growing old and will die before long. I am sure I shall shed one more tear when poor Fidee goes."

A year later, in April 1834, Jud married Sarah Boardman. They moved to Moulmein, and the Wades continued work among the Karen tribes.

Once more Jud had a home. He pastored the church of 84 believers, which grew to 160 members. He

GUESS

1. trained natives to be preachers.
2. worked in the *zayat*.
3. helped people.

While doing all that, Jud translated the Bible into Burmese. In all, he spent

GUESS

1. more than twenty years.
2. more than five years.
3. more than nine years.

Jud began translating Matthew in 1814 and sent the last sheet

105

Jud translated the Bible into Burmese.

of the Bible to the printer in 1840, twenty-six years later.*

During the twelve years Jud and Sarah lived in Moulmein, they had a family of

GUESS	1. six children.
	2. five children.
	3. two children.

The Judsons had four boys and a girl, whose names were Adoniram, Elnathan, Abby Ann, Henry, and Edward.

Sarah was so sick after Edward was born that Mrs. Wade suggested, "Let me take the baby home with me. Henry, too. He is only two and not old enough to help. I'll care for him, too."

Adoniram, eleven, and Elnathan, eight, tried to cook while Abby, only six, did the dishes.

Sarah, however, grew worse. Finally Jud said,

GUESS	1. "We must take her to America."
	2. "I will send her to Calcutta."
	3. "There are doctors in Ava."

Jud, determined to find the best doctors for Sarah, decided to take her and the three older children to America.

In spite of his care, however, Sarah died in the port of St. Helena. Disheartened, Jud continued on to America with his three children.

*In 1985 it was still the only Burmese Bible.

17

Fanny Forester

After thirty-three years, America looked strange to Judson. His ship, the *Sophia Walker*, dropped anchor in Boston Harbor. "Your Aunt Abby is the only person meeting us," Jud told the children. Silently, he added to himself, *My parents and most of my friends, too, are probably dead.* He tweaked little Abby under the chin and said, "I feel like Rip Van Winkle. No one will know us, and we have no place to stay."

But Jud was

GUESS

1. mistaken.
2. upset.
3. correct.

As they stepped off the ship, crowds of people cheered, waved, and tossed streamers. The *Boston Traveller News* had reported his arrival: "America's First Foreign Missionary Returns." A hundred people invited him to their homes.

Adoniram Judson had become

1. a legend.

2. a hero.
3. a well-known name.

Judson was shocked to find many magazines had written about him. A man named Knowles had written a book about Ann after her trip to the United States. Christian people knew of the horrors of Ava and of his translation of the Bible into Burmese. To them it was a story of hair-raising episodes. Thousands of people had prayed and donated money for his support. Now they were to see their hero in person.

The trouble was

GUESS

1. Jud was sick at heart.
2. Jud did not feel like a hero.
3. Jud was shy.

Besides these troubles, Jud's voice failed him. He could only talk in a husky whisper.

He arrived on Wednesday and attended a welcome on Friday at the Bowdoin Square Church in Boston. The crowds appalled him. As he sat on the platform with dignitaries, his

GUESS

1. throat was sore.
2. grief for Sarah haunted him.
3. worry for his children concerned him.

His throat was sore. When he stood up to thank the people for the welcome, his husky whisper could not be heard. William Hague, the pastor, repeated his words as an elderly gentleman made his way to the front.

Suddenly Jud recognized the man. "Samuel Knott!" he cried out. The two men hugged each other as the congregation stared.

"We are the only two survivors of the missionary group of 1812, and I left India in 1816," Sam said to the congregation.

"I'm impressed," he added. "Out of the five who went to India, three are dead. Soon we too will also go, but the Word of God

110

stands fast. We only paved the way for others. Who will take our place? Who will go today?"

After Boston, every church wanted to give Adoniram Judson a welcome service. He was suffocated by visitors.

A week later he took the children and fled north to see the Hasseltines and Sarah's mother and father in Salem.

They took the train. "See the many roads. Those were not built when I left. These canals were not here, and railroads did not link the north and south."

"I heard the railroads will go from the Atlantic to the Pacific," Elnathan said. "I like this country better than Burma."

"It is certainly more healthful," Jud answered.

When they reached Salem, Sarah's mother said, "Going from church to church all over the northeast is no life for children."

"Leave the boys with us," Sarah's relatives begged. "They are a part of our dear Sarah."

Jud decided to

GUESS	1. put the boys in a school.
	2. leave the boys with Sarah's relatives.
	3. take little Abby to his sister.

In the end, Jud heard the boys cry in Worchester and Abby cry in Plymouth when he left them with relatives. "I wish I could avoid all these services and keep the children." He sighed. "But the mission board insists the people want to see me."

In December he was traveling with a pastor, Dr. A. D. Gillette, to Philadelphia for a meeting. A train accident ahead delayed their coach. To pass the time, Dr. Gillette gave Jud

GUESS	1. a game.
	2. a book.
	3. a newspaper.

Dr. Gillette gave Jud a book entitled *Trippings in Author Land* by Fanny Forester.

To be polite Jud riffled the pages. Since the wait was long and

111

there was nothing else to do, he began reading. "The subjects are trivial, but the writing is light and vivid," Jud concluded.

Gillette left Jud when he saw he was reading with interest. When he returned, Jud asked, "Who is Fanny Forester? This writing has great beauty and power."

"Her real name is Emily Chubbock. She was a teacher in a seminary when an editor of the *New York Mirror* read some of her religious writings."

"Oh, she is a Christian? This book doesn't show it," Jud observed.

"Let me tell you about her. A New York editor told her, 'No one will read a poem signed Chubbock; sign it Fanny Forester, and you will see the difference.' "

"What happened?"

"She did sign herself Fanny Forester and began writing what people like to read." Dr. Gillette added, "Now she has skyrocketed to popular fame."

"I should be glad to know her. A lady who writes so well ought to write better. It is a pity she wastes herself on such subjects."

Dr. Gillette smiled and invited Jud to meet Fanny at his home. Jud found Fanny:

GUESS

1. in the kitchen.
2. playing the piano.
3. being vaccinated.

"Fanny Forester" was being vaccinated for smallpox at the moment Dr. Gillette walked in with Jud.

Gillette waited until the doctor finished, and Jud had time to study her silently. She had on a lose morning dress, one arm bared for the doctor. Jud noticed her self-possessed manner and sparkling dark eyes. She couldn't be more than thirty. Her mouth was large and her nose long, but there was life and humor about her. She seemed to find fun—even in a vaccination.

After the introduction, Jud led her to a sofa. "I want to talk to you, young lady," he said.

Emily smiled. "Why sir, I would be delighted and honored!"

Jud told her

1. he enjoyed her book.
2. she should be ashamed of herself.
3. she could write important books.

Jud asked her a question, "As a Christian, how can you employ your noble talents in writing frivolous sketches?"

Emily looked at him. "Your words are harsh, sir, but you radiate warmth and sweetness. I believe you really want to know."

"I do," Jud replied. "I have a reason."

"I was born in poverty. There were twelve children, and we never knew when or if we would eat. I went to work at the age of eleven in a wool factory, piecing ends of broken strands together. I managed to earn enough money to attend the Utica Female Seminary. There I began writing for religious magazines, but my earnings were pitiful until I met an editor who suggested I change my name and write for popular demand."

Jud grinned and said,

| GUESS |

1. "So you sold out!"
2. "So you changed your name."
3. "Money was *that* important?"

"With the money I bought a home for my parents and still keep them in comfort in their old age. Can you blame me?"

"No," Jud admitted. "I do not blame you, but I would like for you to write a book about my wife, Sarah. After Ann's death, Knowles wrote a memoir to her life. I have been thinking that Sarah, too, is worthy of a memoir. Would you write it?"

Emily agreed, and they worked closely together for a month. At the end of that time,

| GUESS |

1. Jud proposed marriage.
2. Jud sent Emily a watch.
3. Emily finished the book.

Jud sent Emily a watch.

On January 20, 1846, Jud wrote a letter to Emily:

"I hand you, dearest one, a charmed blue watch. It always comes back to me and brings its bearer with it. I sent it to Ann when I was in London, and it brought her safely to me. I sent it to Sarah when she was mourning the loss of her husband. Now, I send it to you. You may dash it to pieces—and my heart with it, but I pray it comes back to me with the Emily I love."

It did. They were married and sailed for Burma on July 11, 1846, amidst the good-byes of hundreds, including three tearful children who would be safer in America.

18

The Golden Streets

The voyage was pleasant for Jud and Emily. They laughed and played. Emily was able to draw Judson away from serious meditation to the lighter, more laughable side of life. "The three best doctors are Dr. Diet, Dr. Quiet, and Dr. Merryman," Emily expanded.

Jud was faithful in having

GUESS	1. worship on board every evening. 2. church services on Sunday. 3. Bible study for the crew.

All those meetings were a joy to Jud and Emily.

Emily wrote of the sea: "The water is of inky darkness in the hollows; but each billow, as it bounds upward, becomes green and half transparent, and bursts at the summit, the long wreaths of foam circling over and over each other, tumbling to the bottom, and disappearing like immense piles of down." She ended by writing, "But the beauty of the scene is the showers of rainbows, for the sun is gloriously bright."

Jud listened as she read her descriptions to him. Sometimes his comments were wise and helpful. More often, he laughed in pure delight at her words.

Judson was also writing. From the time he had made his word list of Burmese and English words, he had known that one day he must write a dictionary. "Of course, I felt the translation of the Bible was of first importance. But now that is finished, I must work on the dictionary."

"Why *you?* Why can't someone else do it?" Emily asked.

Jud smiled. "I wish someone else could do it, but

GUESS	1. I've lived here thirty years."
	2. I know the English language."
	3. I know the Burmese language."

Emily had no answer to that. She knew no one else was so qualified. "Will you list the English words first, in alphabetical order, or the Burmese words first?" she asked.

"For a new missionary, the dictionary would be more helpful listing the English first. Later, I can write another one, listing the Burmese words first."

Emily teased Jud. "I guess you are planning to live

GUESS	1. a hundred years."
	2. until this is done."
	3. until tomorrow."

"A hundred years will do nicely, thank you!" Jud agreed.

They discussed locations. "I'm glad we are going to Moulmein where there are Christians," Emily said.

"Yes, living is easier there, but I do feel the call back to Rangoon. I feel the work there is unfinished. Other missionaries won't go because there is no protection by the British."

"Why you, then?"

"I know the people. Let me make a trial trip to see if God wants us there."

Emily said,

1. "Very well."

116

| GUESS |
2. "Moulmein is more healthful."
3. "Rangoon seems dangerous."

Emily said, "Very well."

Once Emily and Judson reached the coast, Christian Burmese met the ship. They took the Judsons up the river to Moulmein in what Emily described as "a long watering trough, whittled to a point at each end." To her nothing was like home—the birds, flowers, vines, or oarsmen, who had "bare, brawny shoulders and turbaned heads."

Emily liked the

| GUESS |
1. strange manners.
2. strange language.
3. strange homes.

Contrasting with the gorgeous pagodas, the homes of the missionaries were plain. Plain teakwood walls only partitioned with screens allowed the circulation of air. Emily said, "I think I was made for an uncivilized land."

She loved Jud and Sarah's boys, Henry and Edward, now four and two years old, and she took them to her heart. Henry said, "My own mamma went away in a boat. Then she got wings and went up. But the boat brought me a new mamma to love me."

Jud, true to his word, went to Rangoon and talked with the city governor, an old acquaintance. Jud told him about the dictionary. "There are learned scholars in Rangoon to help me," he said.

The governor responded,

| GUESS |
1. "You never caused us trouble."
2. "Don't preach to the Burmese."
3. "Remember your services are for foreigners."

The governor agreed. He did not say that Jud should not preach to the Burmese. He simply wanted no trouble.

Jud found an empty second floor with nine rooms. He rented it and returned for Emily and the boys.

Emily named their new home

GUESS	1. Bat Castle.
	2. Beetle Barn.
	3. Ant Heaven.

Jud had not noticed the bats when he rented the place. He told "Green Turban"—Emily's name for the servant—to make the house shine for madam.

"He did make it shine with a vengeance between whitewashing and greasing," Emily lamented. "Our doors and other woodwork are dripping. We can't get rid of the smell, nor is it quite safe to hold too long on the door," she wrote home.

After men worked for a week to rid the place of bats, Emily and Jud could see no difference. Hundreds still stained everything. Bat Castle it remained. Finally they

GUESS	1. put up mosquito curtains.
	2. ignored the bats.
	3. used insect poison.

Finally they put up curtains for ceilings and tried to ignore the bats. The bedbugs were worse. Every crack in the wall housed hundreds. But Emily and Jud were fighters.

On June 2, 1847, Jud and Emily celebrated their first wedding anniversary. Both said it was

GUESS	1. "the happiest year of my life."
	2. "a battle for sure."
	3. "most interesting."

The both said it was the happiest year of their lives.

One thing that made it happy was that both managed to write. Jud progressed from A to E in his dictionary, and Emily finished her book about Sarah Judson. She also wrote several articles about Burma and Christianity.

When Jud tried to find the Christians he had left in Rangoon, he was overjoyed at the progress of some and disheartened by others.

One man said, "It was so hard with no services, no other Christians, and no Bible study. I guess I turned my back on God."

Jud looked at his downcast face. "God is like the sun; the sun warms you when you face it. Yes? But if you turn your back, it still warms you. You are not saved by what you do. God always loves you. Do you still love Jesus?"

"Yes."

"Then turn back to God; He never turned His back on you."

Slowly Christians began visiting Jud. Twos, threes, then dozens came. Toward the end of three months, Jud even dared baptize a new believer.

Then Jud discovered a new danger in the assistant governor. Jud called him

GUESS	1. a ferocious, bloodthirsty monster.
	2. a fiendish cockroach.
	3. a mistaken official.

Jud said the man was a ferocious, bloodthirsty monster because Jud could hear screams of people being tortured in the assistant's courtyard.

On May 29 he learned his house was being watched in order to catch any who were favoring the "Jesus Christ religion." Both Jud and Emily

GUESS	1. hid.
	2. warned the disciples to stay away.
	3. told everyone to come.

Jud warned the disciples to come separately. In spite of the threat, Jud baptized another convert. Within two days

1. the believer was arrested.

119

GUESS

2. the believer was killed.

3. the believer's father was arrested.

The man's father was arrested and brought before the old governor. The charges were dismissed, but the governor let Jud know he would not uphold him again.

A few days later Jud looked at Emily. "My dear, you have become as thin as the shad that went up Niagara."

"I can't keep this food down. I know you always have a good appetite, but poor little Henry says, 'I don't want any dinner.' Even the baby would starve if it were not for the buffalo's milk."

Even Jud became deathly ill. While waiting to recover, he noticed the funeral processions that passed the house every day. When both children were seized by the strange sickness, Jud decided

GUESS

1. to go to Ava.

2. to go to Moulmein.

3. to go to America.

They moved to Moulmein, where Emily Frances was born December 14, 1847.

In Moulmein the British government protected missionaries from persecution.

Jud

GUESS

1. held children's meetings.

2. played games with his boys.

3. worked diligently on his dictionary.

Besides all those things, Jud preached in a long black gown to a congregation of men on one side and women on the other. Sometimes they sang a hymn that Jud composed, "I Long to Reach the Golden Shore."

Emily was busy supervising the boys' education. She finished a set of Scripture questions begun by Sarah. She taught a Bible class and held prayer meetings for Burmese women.

Jud and Emily worked

<table>
<tr><td>GUESS</td><td>1. as though pleasing God.
2. as though they were in a hurry.
3. as though time was short.</td></tr>
</table>

They did all that. In the summer of 1848, Jud became sixty years old. He worked so diligently on his dictionary that he finished the English-Burmese part on January 24, 1849, after ten years of work. "No one can tell what toil it has cost me, but I trust it will be valuable for a long time," Jud said.

Emily said,

<table>
<tr><td>GUESS</td><td>1. "Age seems to improve you."
2. "You work like a galley slave."
3. "You seem to get fat on it."</td></tr>
</table>

Emily said all these things.

It was Jud's habit to walk every morning and evening, but late in September 1849 he caught a cold. It lingered and grew worse. By March he collapsed when he tried to stand up. The doctor recommended a sea voyage.

While they waited for a ship, Jud said to Emily, "I feel I will soon go to the Golden Shore. I wonder what I can give to Jesus, my precious Savior."

"Oh, Jud!" Emily cried. "The things you gave were for others. Can't you see? You paved the way for other missionaries."

"That's true. I wrote tracts so missionaries can give out writings. I translated the Bible so missionaries can give the Word of God to the Burmans.* I wrote the grammar and word list so that new missionaries can learn the language and the dictionary so that they can know the meanings and usage of the Burmese words. But what if no missionaries come?"

*Between 1962 and 1985 the Gideons placed 112,630 Scriptures in Burma.

"Never fear." Emily quieted him. "New missionaries will come."

"How do you know?"

"With God all things are possible. Your faithful life will inspire them," Emily reassured him.

"But, dear, they will forget me when I'm gone!"

"Oh, no. I will write of you. Others will write of you, too. A faithful missionary will *not* be forgotten. Others will be inspired and will follow God."

Adoniram Judson died April 12, 1850. His body was buried at sea, but his soul walked the Golden Shore and the Golden Streets.